Sissi Flegel

Cool Kisses on the Beach

Aus dem Deutschen
von Helena Ragg-Kirkby

Thienemann

From the mountains to the island

"Hey, Mimi, glad I've bumped into you! I was just about to come and see you!"

I turned round. "What's new?"

"Your Abruzzi story was a great success, wasn't it?"

"It was a great trip, too!"

"Of course it was. Do you **fancy** another one? Another trip, I mean."

"Whaaat?"

"Come on, let me take you for a latte."

Markus Fiesel, editor of our daily paper, **headed** straight **for** our favourite café, pulled me down onto the chair next to his, and placed our order.

"It's about the teen pages for September," he explained **without further ado**. "September means the end of the holidays, lots of memories, the start of a new friendship, maybe the end of another. Farewell tears, **wistful** nostalgia, last kisses ... you know what I mean."

"I haven't a clue what you'**re on about**," I said,

---

to fancy – möchten, gern tun; to head for – zugehen auf; without further ado – ohne weitere Umstände; wistful – sehnsüchtig; to be on about sth – von etwas reden

baffled. "Really, I've no idea what you're talking about. Can't you put it more clearly?"

"That's what I'm doing ... Look!" He put a bundle of letters on the table. "This is all fan-mail! Enthusiastic responses to your Abruzzi story! Well, what do you say to that?"

I shook my head, **bemused**. "Does that mean the readers are still talking about my Abruzzi adventure?"

"Exactly!"

"So what sort of things are they writing?"

Markus Fiesel grinned. "Well, you know the stuff: great girl, brave, funny, simply top class. And they want to read more by you."

The drinks arrived and I **took a sip**. I wasn't entirely comfortable with Markus Fiesel's **praise**. "Well, I could write something about school," I said **hesitantly**.

"Yes, of course, later on, in the autumn. But now you've still got two weeks of the holidays, haven't you?"

"Two and a half," I corrected him.

"Well, there you go! You can experience all sorts of things in two and a half weeks. That's why we thought ..."

"Who's 'we'?"

"The editors, who else? We imagined an article: exciting, funny, **lively**. Topic: a girl's island experiences. You get my **drift** – a change of location! From the mountains to an island!"

---

baffled – verblüfft; bemused – verwirrt; to take a sip – einen Schluck trinken; praise – Lob; hesitant – zögernd; lively – lebendig; drift – Absicht

"Aha. And I'm **presumably** supposed to make it all up? I've never been to an island, for goodness' sake. Well, I did once go to Mainau Island and Reichenau Island in Lake Constance. But that's presumably not what you've got in mind, is it?"

"Of course not! If it's going to be an island, it's got to be the coolest, most 'in' island of all. Think about it, Mimi!"

He **inserted** a dramatic pause.

"The coolest, most 'in' island?" I **frowned**. "I've got no idea which one you're thinking of. Mallorca? Madagascar? Mauritius? Tell me which it is, and I'll go and pack my suitcase right away."

"God, Mimi, why does your mind always drift abroad when great things are so close at hand? There are islands in Germany, too! We're thinking of the island to **beat** all islands. Sylt." He grinned expectantly at me. "So, what do you think about that?"

"Nothing."

"Nothing? Why not?"

I took a deep breath. "Markus, I want to become the most famous travel writer ever. I love travelling, I love writing – but what, I ask you, am I supposed to do on Sylt? I've been to Chile, to Canada, to Hong Kong, to Marrakech, to the lonely Abruzzi mountains ... that was travelling, Markus! Not a little **skip** from South Germany to the North Sea. And what's more: Sylt! Isn't that the place where all the people who think they're really someone hang out

---

presumably – vermutlich; to insert – einschieben;
to frown – die Stirn runzeln; to beat – schlagen;
skip – Hüpfer

together? No, Markus, *that* island isn't a place for me. I'd **be better off** on Mainau." I was really starting to warm to my topic, and suggested, "Cycling tour around Lake Constance, boat trip to Mainau – and then: murder in the greenhouse! Attack among the lettuces! **Stabbed** to death by a **leek**!" Now I was the one who was grinning expectantly.

Markus Fiesel was a hard-bitten journalist and grinned back impertinently. "Not bad! I'll think about it. But now back to our suggestion, Mimi. Have you ever thought about how many people can afford a holiday in Mauritius? The flight alone costs a small **fortune**. But you can easily get to Sylt by train, and then you can choose where you want to stay: in the lap of luxury, or in a tent on a campsite."

I **screwed up my nose**. "Well, I've got nothing against tents. But if it rains non-stop, I find it pretty uncomfortable."

"Does that mean you're cancelling the cycling tour to Lake Constance?"

I laughed. "Markus, you know I can't say no to anything that involves the word 'travel'!"

"I thought as much!" Markus put a friendly arm around my shoulders, ordered two more lattes, and then came to the point.

"This is what we'd thought, Mimi: you take the train to Westerland, and then get a taxi to Kampen. One of our **former** colleagues lives there. He **inherited** a Frisian house and lets out two or three

---

to be better off – besser dran sein; to stab – erstechen;
leek – Lauch; fortune – Vermögen;
to screw up one's nose – die Nase rümpfen;
former – ehemalige/-r; to inherit – erben

rooms in summer. You'll stay with him, find out about the island, and he'll put you in touch with the people who know what's what. And by the way," Markus spooned up his **froth**, "it's his idea to ask you if you could write a bit about Sylt."

"His idea? But he doesn't know me!"

Markus Fiesel screwed up his eyes. "As an old hand and former colleague he still has our 'Daily Post' sent to him. He read your piece and thought Sylt would be the perfect place for you now."

"**I don't get it**!"

"No? Then I'll help you on your way," Markus Fiesel said kindly, pulling a folded piece of paper out of his briefcase.

Dear Mimi Muschalek,
*I read your article with great interest, and I've also heard about your travels. Travel is important; travel cultivates the mind (**assuming** one has something in one's mind that can be cultivated!); travel stimulates the imagination; travel awakens us and gives us a keen eye for everything that's different, new, and unusual. But ...*
*REAL ADVENTURES HAPPEN IN THE MIND. Try it out and see if it's true! Come and see us on the island. It's not that far from Stuttgart; it's small and easily navigable by bike. Instead of volcanoes, we have sand dunes; instead of hot geysers we have cold water; instead of **plunging** cliffs, we have sand. Here, we fear dramatic events in nature and human catastrophes. Do come! I'm looking forward to meeting you!*

---

froth – Schaum; I don't get it. – Ich versteh das nicht.; to assume – annehmen; plunging – steil abfallend

"I don't believe it!" I let the note fall onto the table. "Real adventures happen in the mind. What kinds of adventures is he talking about, Markus?"

"That's exactly what you've got to find out, Mimi."

"Hmm. And what if I don't find any?"

"You'll find them."

"Maybe ... And what about Carlos? He'll **have a fit** if I go on my own."

"He can go with you."

"Really?" I **pondered**.

"Of course. A week for the pair of you. You'll stay with Lornsen. Albrecht Lornsen. Deal?"

"I'll have to talk to my aunts first, okay?"

Markus Fiesel knew that my older sister Nicki and I were **orphans**. When our parents – both of them geologists – died in a road accident in Turkey shortly after I was born, our aunts immediately took us in. Since then, they'd been our parents, and we'd been a big happy family with travel in the blood. Aunt Anne is a travel writer and photographer. Aunt Lise takes care of the big house, has the famous green fingers, and writes about cooking and gardening. We love our aunts and understand their **pronounced concern** for our **welfare**.

When I told them about Markus Fiesel's offer, they immediately rang this Herr Lornsen and – naturally! – made sure that we were going to have separate rooms and that he'd treat me like his most treasured possession. When I protested and reminded them of my previous travels, which hadn't

---

to have a fit – einen Anfall bekommen; to ponder – erwägen, nachdenken über; orphan – Waise; pronounced – ausgeprägt; concern – Besorgnis; welfare – Wohlergehen

been without their dangers, Aunt Anne raised a warning finger. "Mimi, there are geographical, geological and climatic dangers. As we know, you're very capable of dealing with those. But you still don't know about human **abysses** yet. We want to protect you from those as long as possible."

"So you think there are human abysses on Sylt?"

Aunt Anne evaded my question. "I probably wouldn't put it quite so **bluntly**, Mimi."

At first, Carlos, like me, screwed up his nose, switched his laptop on and looked to see whether the island had anything to offer, geologically speaking.

"**Crikey**, Mimi! Listen to this: 'The diversity of the coast is the result of simultaneous and successive geological-geomorphological processes in the **Quarternary Period**. Particularly the geomorphological evolution since the Saale ice age around 390,000 years ago ...' Are you listening to me at all? Whatever. I'm coming with you anyway!"

"Oh, great! The geological-geomorphological evolution will get me really excited, too," I mocked, making a card in shocking yellow, **headed**: BEWARE: REAL ADVENTURES HAPPEN IN THE MIND!!!

And so it happened that we packed our rucksacks on Friday, boarded the train on Saturday, arrived in Westerland at around seven that evening, had our hair **tousled** by a **squally** North Sea wind, and stood quarter of an hour later in Kampen outside a **thatched** cottage, ringing the doorbell.

---

abyss – Abgrund; blunt – unverblümt; Crikey! – Mensch!; Quarternary Period – das Quartär; to head – mit einer Überschrift versehen; to tousle – zerzausen; squally – böig, stürmisch; thatched – strohgedeckt

Friendly greeting? No way.

Nobody opened the door.

"Try again," said Carlos.

After the fifth prolonged ring we leaned our rucksacks against the door and walked around the house. My aunt Lise would have been green with **envy** to see the **lush** green lawn. She'd immediately have started exchanging gardening tips over the blooming roses and, what's more, she'd immediately have wanted to know why the house didn't have any **shutters**, as was evidently normal here, to judge by the neighbouring houses.

The **plot** was bordered by a **waist**-high wall made of piled-up stones, which had all sorts of bushes growing on it. Then there were a couple of **stunted** pine-trees and a couple of trees that were standing at such an **angle** that my aunts would undoubtedly have supported them with strong **stakes**. There was nobody in the garden, but the terrace door was open.

"What do you **reckon**? Should we go in?"

---

envy – Neid; lush – satt; shutter – Fensterladen; plot – Grundstück; waist – Hüfte; stunted – verkümmert; angle – Winkel; stake – Pfahl; to reckon – vermuten

"Don't know," replied Carlos uncomfortably. "I'd rather not."

I nodded. "What's more: I'm hungry."

We carried our rucksacks round the back of the house and **deposited** them on the terrace, and then we set off for the village. At the point where two little roads met, we discovered a pub. *The Old Village Pitcher* was its name, and as it was warm and the sun hadn't quite set, all sorts of people were sitting outside and **tucking in**.

"Any idea what a pitcher is?" asked Carlos.

"Course I have – it's something to hold liquids," I explained. "Like milk, or wine, or juice. But here up north the name probably means something different from what it means down south." I frowned. "At home, all the pubs are called 'The Lion', 'The Eagle', 'The Deer', or 'The Linden Tree'."

Carlos raised his shoulders. "What do you expect them to be called here? 'First Dune', 'Second Dune', 'Third Dune'? '*The Old Village Pitcher*' is presumably a pretty imaginative name by local standards."

"Carlos! There aren't any lions where we live either!"

"Oh yes, there are – in the **coat of arms**," he said, **unfazed**, and pulled me inside, as there really wasn't even a tiny space remaining outside.

The lounge was dark because the windows were small and the ceiling was very low. The lounge was packed, so we went to the bar.

"Presumably the only pub in the village," growled Carlos, asking for the menu.

---

to deposit – abstellen; to tuck in – beim Essen zulangen; coat of arms – Wappen; unfazed – ungerührt

"Mornin'", said the man behind the bar. He said it in a very friendly manner and it didn't sound as if he was **pulling our legs**. But he did actually say 'Mornin'', which we translated as 'hello'.

"Good evening!" I said, **taken aback**. After all, it was just before sunset.

Carlos had studied the prices and looked at me **in astonishment**. "Either we starve, or we've got to go and find the nearest McDonald's, Mimi!"

"We can't!" I **wailed**. "I've not eaten a thing apart from the two pretzels with butter since this morning! Isn't there any soup? Or **lentils** and sausages?"

We agreed on the cheapest dish, potato soup with added sausage. While we were waiting, we listened to the man on our left. He was recounting in a booming voice how somebody had been carried out to sea on a **lilo** earlier that day and had alerted everyone to himself and his unfortunate situation by waving to them.

"Well, we stood and watched for a while, then we finally **chugged** out in the motor boat and fetched him in. He wasn't actually in any danger, the water was calm, there wasn't any wind. All harmless, only the guy on the lilo didn't see it like that. His nerves couldn't take any more, I reckon."

I rolled my eyes. Carlos whispered, "Get that, Mimi? Lornsen was right: the lilo swimmer had his adventures in his mind! 'He wasn't in any danger' according to his rescuer."

---

to pull sb's leg – jmdn. veräppeln; taken aback – verblüfft; in astonishment – erstaunt; to wail – jammern; lentil – Linse; lilo – Luftmatratze; to chug – tuckern

We grinned at one another. "How far do the **sharks** come in?" I asked.

The white-haired man with a deep tan had heard me. "In this weather? Depends on the **current**: they stop one or two metres from the shore. But only when they're full!"

Fortunately, our potato soup arrived at that point. The portion was, however, intended for people on a diet-trip: ten spoonfuls at most, and then the little cup was empty.

After we'd **amicably** shared the last piece of bread, my neighbour **nudged** me. "New to the island? The sea air makes you hungry."

He laughed so heartily that the little lounge wobbled, and I stared at the plates and bowls that were just being carried back into the kitchen, my tummy rumbling. The leftovers would cheerfully have satisfied Carlos and me.

"I wonder whether Lornsen's got home in the meantime?" I asked. "I mean, he knows when we're arriving!"

As his cottage wasn't far from the *Village Pitcher*, we walked back. "Damn! He's still not home!" I **cursed**. "Come on, let's find out the way to the beach. Nothing beats a refreshing swim!"

We dug out our swimming things and towels, stuffed the whole lot into a plastic bag, and asked for the quickest way there. "Go along Alte Dorfstraße to the traffic lights. That way," explained a man who was just coming out of the next-door house, pointing his stick in the direction of the sunset.

---

shark – Hai; current – Strömung; amicably – freundschaftlich; to nudge – anstupsen; to curse – fluchen

"Blimey, Mimi, that wasn't one of our most brilliant moments," said Carlos. "If you think of the map, the water is quite clearly in the west. And where does the sun **set**?"

"In the west," I answered like a good girl. "Carlos! There's a bakery here!"

I ran off, bought a bag of '**barm cakes**' and offered a roll to Carlos. "It's almost incredible how differently the people here talk. They say 'mornin'' for evening, call bread rolls barm cakes and, if I'm not mistaken, the road Lornsen's house is in is called Sjipwai – whatever that's supposed to mean. And the weirdest thing is that we're still in our own country!"

"Yeah, yeah, true adventures!" **teased** Carlos.

We strolled up Alte Dorfstraße and stopped at the traffic lights. "Terrible! Absolutely terrible!" stated Carlos. "If they hadn't installed traffic lights here, we'd never cross the road! 'A never-ending stream of cars'. That's what it always says in the books, isn't it?"

"Yeah," I agreed, chewing.

We'd barely crossed the road and gone a little way down towards the dunes when it turned deathly quiet and **devoid of** humans, although we could see a campsite to our right.

A few moments later the sea was lying before us.

We took our sandals off, Carlos reached for my hand, and together we raced downhill. What do I mean, 'downhill'! It was down the dunes that we raced!

---

to set – *hier:* untergehen; barm cake – Brötchen; to tease – necken; devoid of – ohne

At the bottom, where the sand was firm, I **flung my arms round Carlos' neck**. "That was brilliant!"

We kissed – and when I opened my eyes again, I was left **gasping**. Four men, all **stark** naked, were walking past us. I swallowed. "Carlos –"

But Carlos didn't respond. He was looking, **spellbound**, to his right, and I saw that his eyes were almost popping out of his head. "For goodness' sake, shut your mouth! It's totally **indecent** to **gawp** at a naked girl to that extent," I snapped, shaking him violently. "Hey! Carlos! I'm here! Your Mimi!"

Carlos turned red. "Did you see that? I think everyone here is naked," he **croaked**. "Unbelievable!"

I looked around. "Not everyone, just almost everyone. Should we ... What do you reckon? Do you want to go swimming without your swimming trunks, too?"

Carlos scratched his chin. "I'm not really sure ... Or do you want to?"

"Nah. It's all a bit sudden. Hey, do you think we missed a sign saying '**Nudist Beach**'?"

"Don't think so. But I do think they should put one up so that strangers like us are prepared for it. I have to say, that girl just now ..."

"Just one girl?" I teased. "That's nothing. The first thing I saw was four naked men, Carlos! I have to **digest** that one first!"

---

to fling your arms round sb's neck – jmdm. die Arme um den Hals schlingen; to gasp – nach Luft schnappen; stark – völlig; spellbound – gebannt; indecent – unanständig; to gawp – angaffen; to croak – krächzen; nudist beach – FKK-Strand; to digest – verdauen

"Oh God, Mimi! Do you really want to go swimming?"

"Course I do. I've bought a new bikini specially. It has to be **christened** and worn; I can't afford a bad investment."

Carlos grinned, relieved. "Seems like the people here don't have enough money to buy decent swimsuits, hey?"

We got changed in the dunes and then very quickly discovered that the water was pretty chilly.

"Yes, but if you throw yourself into the waves, it's warm!" cried Carlos, pulling me with him.

It was just brilliant. We swam out a way, let the waves carry us back to the beach, then swam back out again. Then Carlos pulled me down under the water. I **emerged**, swam after him, planning to do the same to him, but not likely! He was so much stronger than me that I, unfortunately, swallowed a big **gulp** of water, which delayed my ability to **swear revenge**. But revenge was what I'd get – I was quite sure of that!

It came earlier than we expected. As we made our way out of the water, gasping and out of breath, and went over to our clothes, a Superwoman jogged past us. She looked like a character from an advert: legs that went on for ever, long, blonde, flowing hair ... Carlos was completely **bowled over**. Red-faced, he watched her go until I put my hands over his eyes.

"Do you think I find it amusing when you're con-

---

to christen – einweihen; to emerge – auftauchen; gulp – Schluck; to swear – schwören; revenge – Rache; to be bowled over – sprachlos sein stantly gawping at every pair of bouncing breasts you see?" I snapped.

"Crikey, Mimi, I just have to get used to this beach a bit," he defended himself.

"Well, get on with it, okay? It's about time you thought about the geological-geomorphological **faults**! Okay?"

We'd got dressed and were facing one another angrily, plastic bag and sandals in our hands. As I was just about to reach my hand out in **reconciliation**, the Superwoman jogged back. Funny – such a short route? Ten metres there, ten metres back? There had to be a reason for that one.

And there was a reason. He was sitting right next to the jogging route, and everything he'd spread out around himself looked expensive, exclusive and fine: the bathing towel, the bag, the shoes and all sorts of other **bits and bobs**.

"You're too late, Carlos," I said, pointing my chin towards the man sitting there. "But you'd never have been able to keep up with her anyway."

Carlos swallowed. "Probably a little Wanda, hey?"

"Carlos!" I yelled, putting my arms around his neck. "You really have **twigged**!"

Wanda was the name of the creature who'd first of all flung herself **mercilessly** at Carlos in Morocco before dropping him like a hot potato when she met an older, richer guy. Carlos hadn't wanted to listen to me then. It was only once it was almost too late – at the very last minute, so to speak – that he'd

---

fault – *hier:* Verwerfung; reconciliation – Versöhnung; bits and bobs – Kleinkram; to twig – kapieren; merciless – gnadenlos

realized that Wanda was just using him as way to pass the time and as an object to practise on. It had been a heavy **blow** to his **vanity**.

Now he put his arm around me. We tramped back through the sand to the top of the dunes until we came to the place where the path began. There we turned and looked down at the water.

The sun had set; the cloudless sky extended in a deep, dark blue across the sea, which was almost black. The waves ran quietly and evenly onto the beach, leaving bits of white froth which **dissolved** and were replaced, dissolved and formed anew ...

As we stood there watching, the moon arose from the water.

Carlos pulled me to him. I could feel his heart beating and could hear his breath and that of the sea. We didn't move from the spot. For an eternity, we watched the moon, shimmering like a **mother-of-pearl** button, gliding higher and higher into the blue-black sky. We'd never felt so close to one another. Neither of us wanted to break the **spell**.

This was eventually done for us by a couple of people in whose way we were standing. We stepped aside and I whispered, "Look, Carlos, we don't have to go back the same way to the village. There's a way through the dunes here."

After we'd stumbled several times over **tangled weeds** and grasses, we preferred to walk in single file and soon discovered that we had in fact ended up back in the village and in Kurhausstraße.

---

blow – Schlag; vanity – Eitelkeit; to dissolve – sich auflösen; mother-of-pearl – Perlmutt;
spell – Zauber; tangled – verwickelt; weed – Kraut

At the next opportunity we turned off to the left and found ourselves in another street that took Carlos' breath away. Or, rather, it wasn't the street, but the cars that were parked there. "Mimi," he gasped. "Mimi! Look at that sports car! The latest model! And that one there! Wow, that has to be **custom-built**!"

Cars leave me pretty cold. Of course, I didn't even have a driving licence yet. But the shops that the cars were parked outside were just amazing as well: I'd never in my life seen so many **posh** labels in such a small area.

But the thing that totally **flabbergasted** us was something completely different. Set back a bit and pretty much at the end of the road, we found a pub. At home it would say "beer garden in the yard behind the pub", and the beer gardens are mostly pretty **cosy** places. With old **chestnut-trees** which drop their fruits into your glass in autumn, or with other trees that offer you shade, and which have birds twittering in their branches.

Here, the yard was in front of the pub. We noticed little decorative ornamental trees in posh tubs, and a **crush** of happy people. And who did I spot at the front?

"Carlos! Can you see her?"

"Who? Look, Mimi, I've only ever seen this model in *Cars, Motoring and Sport*. Heavenly, don't you think?"

"The car?"

---

custom-built – spezialangefertigt; posh – vornehm; flabbergasted – verblüfft; cosy – gemütlich; chestnut-tree – Kastanienbaum; crush – Masse, Menge

"What else?"

"Oh, Carlos! You're so sweet! Haven't you spotted Wanda the Second yet?"

"Wanda the Second? Who's that supposed to be? Wow, that thing has extra wide tyres! And **hub-caps**, they have to –"

"Okay. Don't move."

It was the long-legged blonde jogger from the beach. She had a glass in her hand and was **hell-bent on** flirting with that guy ... with *that* guy? No, it was more like *those* guys. Mimi, I said to myself, pay attention: you'll learn a life-skill here!

Carlos suddenly grabbed my arm. "Hey, Mimi, that guy over there's **giving you the come-on**. Come on, let's go, I don't like it."

"I've not even noticed it," I said. "But you know what? The blonde girl from the beach is much younger than I'd thought. My age. More like seventeen than eighteen. Carlos! You don't need to drag me around after you! I'm not your prisoner!"

"Sorry!" He let me go. "That guy really **bothered** me. The way he stared at you – honestly!"

I giggled, then started laughing. "The things we've experienced since we arrived, Carlos! It's unbelievable!"

Carlos hadn't found his good mood yet. "Mimi, if this Albrecht Lornsen isn't back yet, I'll start to get seriously worried. He's either forgotten about us, or something's happened to him. Do you know if there's a youth hostel anywhere in the village?"

---

hub-cap – Radkappe; hell-bent on – versessen auf;
to give sb the come-on – jmdn. anmachen;
to bother – lästig sein, Sorgen machen

"Carlos! All these questions! Just wait and see first whether Lornsen's in before you start **doing your head in**!"

"Well, okay ... But Mimi, if he's not there, all we can afford is a bed in a youth hostel. When I think of the price of the potato soup ..."

"I said you shouldn't start thinking yet, Carlos!"

For the third time that evening, we were standing outside Lornsen's door. I reassured Carlos with a quick kiss, then pressed the bell.

A light went on, and we heard a voice: "I'm coming!" The door was pulled open, someone said, "Welcome!" – and then a huge, hot, **damp**, slobbery tongue licked my face.

The dog that it belonged to had put his front **paws** on my shoulders and was completely **impervious to** my pushing and shoving.

"Resistance is **futile**," said the voice, laughing, and then I heard an energetic, "Noballs, sit!"

The tongue wiped my face once more, then the **mutt** removed his paws and trotted into the house as **meekly** as a lamb.

"Wh-why is that giant called Snowball?" I asked, fishing a tissue from my trouser pocket. "He's got dark **fur**, brown, almost black."

"The dog isn't called Snowball. He had to be castrated when he was younger, so we called him 'Noballs' – No **balls**. Get it? But come on in now. I've been expecting you for ages."

---

to do one's head in – sich den Kopf zerbrechen; damp – feucht, paw – Pfote; impervious to – unzugänglich für; futile – sinnlos; mutt – Köter; meek – sanft; fur – Fell; balls – Eier/Hoden

"Expecting us?" I repeated **indignantly**. "We've already stood outside your door twice!"

"Oh? Really? Sit down, I'll be back in a second. I'm just going to fetch the tea-tray. We drink tea at all times of the day or night here, you see."

I had, meanwhile, started to have all kinds of **reservations**. Hadn't Marcus Fiesel said that Albrecht Lornsen was retired? How could that be? He'd been expecting us, and still hadn't been at home? That didn't match up with our concept of **hospitality**. It was in fact a pretty rude way to behave, wasn't it? Hopefully, the man wasn't completely gaga ...

Herr Lornsen put the tray on a little table near his armchair and said, "So, you're Mimi then. And you must be Carlos, eh? My name is Albrecht. How would you like your tea? With cream and sugar?"

"As it is. Nothing in it, thanks."

"That's how I drank it at the start as well. We'll see how it tastes to you by the end of the week ... And what have you discovered since you got here?" he suddenly asked.

Albrecht must have added something to the tea to make us talkative. We told him about the **hefty** prices, the nudists on the beach and the people outside the pub, and Carlos, of course, described all the cars in their great **splendour**.

We left out the business with the moon. That belonged to just the two of us.

---

indignant – verärgert; reservation – *hier:* Vorbehalt; hospitality – Gastfreundschaft; hefty – heftig; splendour – Pracht

"You no doubt thought I was a forgetful, old fool," Albrecht finally said. "Senile and **inhospitable**."

I felt myself turning red, as that was precisely what I had thought.

Albrecht gave me a rather cheeky grin. "I may be old, senile and forgetful. But I'm not inhospitable. You see, I was just testing you."

"What was a test?" asked Carlos uncomprehendingly.

"My absence," Albrecht replied coolly.

Markus Fiesel really was mean. He ought to have warned me about Albrecht. "If you weren't there," I said rather **curtly**, "you couldn't remotely test us."

"Oh yes, I could!"

"How, then?"

Albrecht raised his hand and counted on his fingers. "Firstly: the patio door wasn't locked. Even so, you didn't go into the house. You put your rucksacks by the door."

"You don't just walk into strange houses," I said.

"No, that's not good manners. But some people would have used my absence as the perfect opportunity to **have a snoop around**."

I shrugged my shoulders. "That's what some people are like."

"But you, fortunately, aren't among them," Albrecht remarked. "You were hungry, you found the only baker, you experienced and survived the shock on the beach without **coming to blows**. Congratulations! I'm glad you're my guests!"

---

inhospitable – nicht gastfreundlich; curt – barsch;
to have a snoop around – herumschnüffeln;
to come to blows – sich streiten

I was still **cross**. "Do you test all your guests? I mean, that's a bit like snooping, isn't it?"

Albrecht shook his head. "The thing is, I only rent the rooms out in emergencies, so I'm not dependent on the income. And, Mimi, I've got to support you in your investigations. But are you **worth** supporting? That was the question."

"*That* question," Carlos suddenly said, "*that* question is one I could have answered for you. Mimi's always worth supporting."

Albrecht was so surprised that he **choked**, coughed terribly, but finally **panted**, "You, too, Carlos!"

I finally looked around. The room was tiny, and the walls were **glazed in** bluey-white tiles. A picture hung above the fireplace, **depicting** a boat with several sails. It was somehow different from the pictures I was familiar with. I stood up. "That's a real model ship in a glass case!"

Albrecht nodded. "It's a copy of the ship that belonged to one of the last **whalers** on the island. Peter Eschels was his name. His **schooner** – that's what this kind of ship is called – froze solid in the ice of Greenland. They set off across the ice with three gigs – they're rowing boats – and 23 captured walruses in order to find other ships and to get to safety. With an incredible amount of effort, they dragged the gigs over the bumpy ice and finally left them behind after trekking for 19 days. Equipped with only the bare necessities, they carried on, fi-

---

to be cross – sauer sein; to be worth – etwas wert sein; to choke – keine Luft bekommen; to pant – keuchen; to be glazed in – verkleidet sein mit; to depict – darstellen; whaler – Walfänger; schooner – Schoner

nally coming upon broken ice on the 22nd day and rowing to land on an **ice floe**. There they came upon a house in which they found, to their shock and horror, the **corpses** of 18 frozen seamen whose ship was lying in a pretty damaged state by the shore. They made it seaworthy again and, after they had been locked into the ice for 47 days, sailed away and successfully reached Hammerfest in Norway."

"When did that happen? And why did you hang up this of all pictures?" I wanted to know.

"Peter Eschels is a very, very distant relative," replied Albrecht. "After this adventure he didn't go whaling again – the golden days were, in any case, already over – instead he travelled the seas of the world on **merchant** ships. His ship **capsized** by the English shore. That was in 1852. Peter was 48 years old then."

"That was a pretty dangerous job," said Carlos thoughtfully. "And your relative didn't live to be very old either."

Albrecht nodded in agreement.

"What did you mean by 'the golden days were, in any case, already over'?" I wanted to know.

"In the 15th and 16th centuries, the local population lived mainly from catching **herring** and **cod**," explained Albrecht. "But when the **stock** was decimated, the fishermen switched over to whaling. In 1777 around 270 seamen lost their lives: the risky job of hunting whales in the **drift-ice** around

---

ice floe – Eisscholle; corpse – Leiche;
merchant – Handels-, Händler; to capsize – kentern;
herring – Hering; cod – Kabeljau; stock – Bestand;
drift-ice – Treibeis

Greenland turned out to be their **doom**, for the sharp-edged, massive ice-floes crushed their ships. In the 19th century the supply of whales had reduced so much that most fishermen signed up with merchant ships. By the way, one of the island fêtes is supposed to **hark back to** the dangerous practice of whaling. The Biikebrennen, or burning of heaps of **driftwood**, was the farewell party for the seamen. Or at least that's what some people say. I don't believe it, though. Our ancestors always lit such fires everywhere during the winter **solstice**."

I **yawned furtively**. These whaling stories really were thrilling, but after the long journey and the exciting evening I was pretty tired.

"I'll show you your rooms now," said Albrecht. "And tomorrow, above all else, you must meet Tom Thoms. But I shan't tell you any more for now!"

Was my room ever tiny! I reckon my rucksack was the biggest thing in the whole room. The bed was a narrow, **oblong** box built under the angle of the roof. The greatest bit about it was that there was a blue checked curtain in front of it that I could close. I snuggled down into the bed and discovered that I could touch the **timber** above with my head and below with my feet. I wondered whether Carlos' bed was any longer? I hoped it was, or the poor thing would have to sleep with his legs drawn up!

---

doom – Verhängnis, Schicksal; to hark back to – zurückgehen auf; driftwood – Treibholz; solstice – Sonnenwende; to yawn – gähnen; furtive – verstohlen; oblong – rechteckig; timber – Holz

Holly

\- = - = -

In the morning I awoke rested and ready to get going. I jumped out of my box-bed, banged my head against the **beams**, cursed quietly and had a shower. Wow, Mimi, I thought, how times change! That time in Chile I'd been **utterly** ashamed because Carlos had seen me standing at the window in that unspeakably embarrassing nightshirt. I was crying my eyes out because of Rory, the unfaithful **creep** who I had thought was in love with me! And now? Now I was on Sylt with Carlos!

I put on my best jeans and my favourite pinky-orange shirt. **Admittedly**, it took a bit of getting used to. The colours were pretty **strident**, but I thought it suited me better than anything else.

Then I tied up my hair (no, not long, silky and golden, but brown and **frizzy**) with three hair-bobbles in pink, orange and denim blue, all wrapped around one another. I put mascara on, applied lip-gloss – and was ready for my first day on the island.

Albrecht was single; that much I knew from

---

beam – Deckenbalken; utterly – total; creep – Widerling; admittedly – zugegebenermaßen; strident – schrill; frizzy – kraus

Markus Fiesel. He had a housekeeper who inhabited the kitchen. She was called Märthe, was small and **stout**, and her face was full of laughter lines. She had prepared a **sumptuous** breakfast and was **shovelling** eggs, bacon and fried mushrooms onto our plates, with the bread-basket on the side. Carlos came crashing down the stairs, gave me a good morning kiss, and then Albrecht came shuffling along, too. I hadn't realized at all yesterday how small, grey-haired and **mischievous** he was – he looked in fact like an ageing friendly magician from a fantasy story.

"I'm **grumpy** in the mornings," he said. "You can talk to me when I've had my third cup of coffee."

Carlos and I grinned. In no time at all we had polished off the eggs and were spreading our '**rounds**' with butter and strawberry jam.

Someone was missing. Of course: that mutt Noballs!

"So where's the dog?" I asked.

As if I'd called him, claws scratched at the wood at that very moment. The door was pushed open and Noballs came trotting over to me. He put his head on my **lap** and looked **soulfully** into my eyes.

"Are you hungry? Haven't you had anything to eat yet?" I asked sympathetically.

"Him?" Märthe laughed and told us something in her dialect which we only understood fragments of.

---

stout – füllig; sumptuous – üppig; to shovel – schaufeln;
mischievous – schelmisch, verschmitzt;
grumpy – mürrisch; round – *hier:* Brotscheibe;
lap – Schoß; soulful – seelenvoll

Albrecht giggled and Märthe put her hand over her mouth. "Try it," Albrecht told her.

Märthe did him the favour for better or for worse. "Noballs wants to beg for his second breakfast. But don't give him anything, or you'll never get rid of him!"

"But he looks so hungry!"

"He's a perfect actor," growled Albrecht. "'Dog **battling** with starvation' is his favourite act."

I found it difficult to resist those **pleading** eyes. "Go and see your master," I told him. But he **waddled off** to Carlos and licked his shoes clean.

"So, now I've downed my coffee," Albrecht suddenly declared. "Off you go, my dears. There are two bikes waiting for you outside. You can use them to go to Wenningstedt. Here's a map of the island. You go down the Alte Dorfstraße, cross the road at the traffic lights, and turn onto the cycle track. Got it? In Wenningstedt, go to the village pond. That's where my best friend lives; Tom Thoms is his name. If he's not at home – you never know what he's got planned – his daughter Elli will be there. Elli runs a guest-house. Oh yes, and there's something else. Elli's daughter is called Holly. I like her."

"Okay. And what are we supposed to do at Tom Thoms' house?" I asked.

Albrecht simply spooned strawberry jam out of the jar – my aunt Lise would have had a heart attack!

"What are you supposed to do there? He's got a whole supply of the best stories about the island.

---

to battle – kämpfen; to plead – inständig bitten; to waddle off – davonwatscheln

But how am I supposed to know what you're interested in? No idea. So ask him yourself what you want to know."

Astonished, I made no reply. I'd have liked to say, "How am *I* supposed to know what I want to ask?" But as the **budding** best travel journalist of all time, it's better not to ask such questions. That's unprofessional. Totally uncool.

So I said "Okay" for the second time that morning, stood up and waited impatiently for Carlos to empty his cup.

Albrecht went into the next room and returned with a little package which he pressed into my hand. "Little present for the journalist-to-be," he explained. "A notebook like the ones that famous writers use. You'll get something from me, too, Carlos. I just don't know yet what it's going to be because I don't know you well enough." He laughed. "But it would be the first time that nothing **suitable** occurred to me!"

The weather looked pretty undecided, so we quickly fetched our anoraks and rode off: on **genuine vintage** models with back-pedal brakes and three **gears**!

Wenningstedt is the village south of Kampen. You need, in vintage bike terms, at the most three-quarters of an hour to reach it. You can't miss the village pond either, as it's right next to the church, which is built of dark red brick.

We rang the bell where we saw the name *Thoms*

---

astonished – erstaunt; budding – angehend; suitable – passend, geeignet; genuine – echt; vintage – alt; gear – Gang

in small letters and *Dune View Guest-House* in very large ones – and waited.

"We've presumably got to pass another test," I grumbled, ringing the bell for a second time.

Now we could hear quite a lot of bumping and banging, then the door was pulled open and a girl of my age was standing in front of us. I immediately liked her; Carlos told me later that he also found her all right.

"Yes?" the girl asked.

"You must –" I stammered, "are you Holly?"

"Why? Do you want a room? Bad luck, they're all occupied." The girl was damned energetic. And **spirited**. And she looked fabulous. Simply fantastic. Foreign. Exotic. She had skin like latte, black eyes, and long, black, wavy hair in two **plaits**.

"Hey, we don't want a room. We've already got rooms. We want to visit Tom Thoms. Apparently he's your grandfather, so Albrecht Lornsen said."

Holly **beamed at us**. "**Well, I never!** You must be Mimi and Carlos, right? Albrecht said you were coming! Come in, come on!"

She led us into the kitchen that, a few pots and pans aside, looked exactly like Albrecht's kitchen.

"Tea? Coffee?" Without waiting for an answer, Holly filled two gigantic cups with coffee, spooned sugar in, added milk, and put them in front of our noses.

"So: my grandfather isn't here today. He might not be back tomorrow either. If we're lucky, he'll be

---

spirited – lebhaft; plait – Zopf; to beam at sb – jmdn. anstrahlen; Well, I never! – Na so was!

back the day after tomorrow. **Funerals** so often end up as cheerful parties, don't you find? What I mean by that is: during the holidays I help my mother with her work. I make beds, clean the basins, vacuum, the usual stuff. I'll be done in quarter of an hour, then I'll have time for you. Okay?"

"F-f-fine," stammered Carlos. "Albrecht did say your grandfather –"

"Hey, he's at an old friend's funeral. I said, didn't I? Over on Amrum. Nobody knows when he's coming back. So I'll take over his job, okay?"

I suddenly had to laugh.

"What's wrong?"

"Albrecht said he liked you! Now I know why!"

"Oh?"

"Yes! You're kind of turbo-charged. It's fantastic!"

"Must be because of my Jamaican great-great-grandmother," said Holly. "All my male ancestors up until my grandfather ..."

"The one who's at the funeral?" I asked.

"Exactly. All the ones until him were merchants and ..."

"... whalers," Carlos interrupted.

"Well, you do know a lot about me," remarked Holly. "In that case you no doubt know that my **aforementioned** great-great-grandfather brought back a woman from Jamaica with him? He wasn't married then, so there was nothing wrong with it."

"We'd never have guessed such a thing," said Carlos, acting shocked.

"Good for you, I –"

---

funeral – Beerdigung;
aforementioned – zuvor schon erwähnt

"Holly! Where are you?" someone called.

"My mother," explained Holly. "Wait here in the kitchen, I'll be quick, okay?"

We didn't have to wait long. Holly returned with her mother Elli as well as buckets, **scrubbing brushes** and cloths of all kinds and sizes. "I can go now," she said breathlessly. "What do you want to see? Experience? Get to know? Birds? Plants? Places?"

"People, sea – and stuff," I quickly said.

"Good, that suits me. I suggest we call in at the hotel called *Behind the Dunes* first. One of the best hotels on Sylt. My friend Maike works there as a chambermaid during the holidays. I'm sure she'd be able to sort you out with a whole pile of great stories."

Her mother nodded in agreement. "That's a good idea. It is quite a way by bike, but –"

"Mother! The ride is a pleasure in this fantastic weather!" cried Holly.

Fantastic weather? We'd have called it a '**dismal** day' at home.

We pedalled off without asking where the hotel was: we simply didn't get round to it.

Holly shot ahead like **lightning**. I was in pretty good shape, but the sandy paths that Holly favoured as short cuts demanded my full attention. Carlos followed me – until he gave a yell and plunged into the **heather**.

"It's nothing," he quickly assured me, taking care to make sure that Holly didn't realize what had happened. Men!

---

scrubbing brush – Scheuerbürste; dismal – trüb, düster; lightning – Blitz; heather – Heidekraut

Unfortunately, I pretty quickly **ran out of puff**. With my last bit of strength I yelled, "Holly! Stop for a minute!"

"What's wrong? Are you **worn out**?"

"Rubbish! But when you dash around the place, I don't get to see anything of it at all! I want to see something! I don't want to set records!"

"Fine. Yes, you're right," cried Holly, turning back. "I don't like riding at a **leisurely pace**; I find it makes you so tired. What's more, I know the path."

"Exactly!" I panted.

We cruised along more slowly. There wasn't much to see in the area: **expanses** of sky, moorland and **pastures** – but despite that, and inexplicably enough, I thought it was lovely. I wondered what made it so special, but before I could reach any conclusion, we had reached a village. The yellow sign said "Keitum," and we followed the white signposts to the hotel. We rode along a long, gravelled drive, then jumped off our bikes.

"Where's Maike?" Holly asked the girl on reception.

"Maike? Today's her day off."

"Bad luck," commented Holly, disappointed. "What shall we do now?" One of her plaits had come undone. She combed her black waves with her fingers and **re-plaited** her hair. "Well, maybe we'll meet someone at the pool. Come on."

By now, the sun was blinking through the clouds, so perhaps the pool wasn't at all a bad idea.

---

to run out of puff – außer Atem kommen; to be worn out – erschöpft sein; leisurely – gemächlich; pace – Tempo; pasture – Weide; to re-plait – neu flechten

Johanna

We wandered behind the building. The garden – or, rather, the park – was so arranged that it would have made my aunt Lise **swoon. Canopied wicker beach chairs** stood all the way round the pool, and several guests were in fact stretching their faces up into the tired sun.

Carlos suddenly grabbed hold of me. "Mimi, over there ... isn't that the jogging girl from Kampen beach?"

"Where? Oh, there ... Crikey, Carlos, it is her!"

"Have you seen someone you know?" asked Holly.

"We don't know her. We've just seen that blonde girl before. Yesterday evening in Kampen."

The girl was sitting on a mat. Next to her, a boy was **dangling** his legs into the water.

"Hi," said Holly, installing herself in front of the pair. "How are you? How are things?" She sat down. "Do you want to meet my friends? Mimi and Carlos. I'm Holly. And what are your names?"

"That was the fastest **chat-up** I've ever seen in my

---

to swoon – ohnmächtig werden; canopied – überdacht; (wicker) beach chair – Strandkorb (aus Rattan); to dangle – baumeln; chat-up – Anmache

life," Carlos murmured next to me. "I need to take note, Mimi."

"Of course, Carlos!" I grinned at him. "I reckon they're not exactly delighted by our company."

"Hmm. Not the girl, but the boy might be a bit keener."

"So, come on!" Holly shouted to us.

The boy laughed. "I'm Constantin!"

"Hi!"

"Hi!"

The girl still hadn't said anything.

"So, what about you? Have you got a name, or could your parents not agree on one when you were born?" Holly **persisted**.

"She's called Johanna," Constantin answered for her.

"You're **disturbing** us," said Johanna.

Well, she could have put it even more bluntly. "You're disturbing us" was pretty mild when you saw how furious her face was when she said it.

Constantin raised his eyebrows. "Rubbish," he said unexpectedly firmly. "You're not disturbing us at all. Quite the opposite! Are you staying here, too?"

"No." Holly shook her head. "I've been looking for a friend who's got her day off."

"What? Your friend works here?" Johanna wanted to know.

"Some people have to work for a living," Holly explained cheerfully. "To be honest, I'd be pretty bored if I didn't work."

"What kind of work do you do?" asked Johanna.

"I'm actually still at school, but I help my

---

to persist – bestehen auf; to disturb – stören

mother in the holidays. We've got a guest-house in Wenningstedt. And what do you do when you're not on holiday, Johanna?"

"I'm starting at university soon. Studying History of Art. Or Architecture. I don't know yet. I'm doing my **'A' levels** in a year's time." She put her hand on Constantin's leg.

"Then you're the same age as me," I said.

"Really? I thought you were older than me."

Wow, that hit home! Nobody had ever said that I looked old! I gasped for air.

Holly had most probably noticed, as she changed the subject. "What about you, Constantin? Are you passing the time with your girlfriend?"

"How do you come up with that nonsense?" he asked, **dumbfounded**.

"Well, because Johanna **worships** you as if you were that **gorgeous** guy from the Levi's advert. That's why! Although –" Holly put her head on one side and smiled. "Although you'd probably make a great mate – Johanna aside."

"How am I supposed to take that?"

Holly giggled and said with a meaningful look at Johanna, "Tell me who you go around with, and I'll tell you who you are!"

Constantin laughed. "Crikey, Holly, that's what my father drilled into me every other day!"

Johanna stood up. She stretched and tossed her long hair back, then dipped her big toe into the water, saying, "Hey, Constantin, I'm off. See you this evening?"

'A' levels – Abitur; dumbfounded – verblüfft;
to worship – anbeten; gorgeous – großartig

"Don't know. Maybe. Where will I find you?"

"Same place, same time: in the *Malabar*." Johanna reached for her swimming towel. "What about you lot? Don't you poor people have to work this evening?"

"I'm always working," I said **casually**.

"Me, too," Carlos supported me.

"Oh yes? So what do you do?" Johanna looked at him closely. Guaranteed, she was noticing that my Carlos was wearing jeans with no designer label, and a pretty worn-out polo shirt. And his shoes weren't **up to much** either. She had quite rightly **got him down as** a poor penniless devil; she screwed up her nose and asked **cattily**, "Are you still at school, or do you also work in the hotel trade?"

"Neither – nor," replied Carlos. "I'm a student. Nothing particular; a bit of this, a bit of that. Mainly ... but there's no way it would interest you, Johanna."

"Quite right. I have other interests. See you then!"

"See you!"

"Wow!" said Holly. "That is one creature. What do you like so much about her, Constantin?"

"Nothing. Goodness knows where I met her," he replied, shaking his head. "She probably met me. Somehow, she was suddenly just there."

"Are you on your own?"

"No, I'm here with my mother. Don't get me wrong. It's just that my father died a couple of months ago. I didn't want to ... my mother ... I wanted –"

---

casual – lässig; to not be up to much – nicht viel taugen; to get sb down as – jmdn. abstempeln als; catty – giftig

"No need to explain," Holly quickly interrupted him. "It's obvious that you have to accompany your mother. But why did you come to Sylt? Was there a reason for it?"

Constantin nodded. "She met my father here. By the way, she's coming over."

He jumped up and ran towards her, then came back and said, "Tonight in the *Malabar*, okay? See you then!"

"So, we've done here. Come on, I'll show you something else of the island!" Holly promised.

The first sight was the Keitum Church of St Severin. "There's supposed to have been a shrine to Odin here in **Teutonic** times," explained Holly. "Odin was a **pagan** god. Well, when the island was converted by missionaries, they built a chapel on the earlier site. It was practical because the people didn't have to get used to a lot of new things. The church tower was added later so that the **seafarers** could **get their bearings**."

We also walked through the **graveyard** which, with its old trees and carefully **pruned** bushes, looked like a park, and then cycled further. At first we went in a westerly direction, then Holly turned sharply off towards the south. After a while she stopped and said that she wanted to go out to the southern tip of the island to show us the paradise of birds there.

"Is that okay by you?"

"Why not?" replied Carlos.

Teutonic – germanisch; pagan – heidnisch; seafarer – Seefahrer; to get one's bearings – sich orientieren; graveyard – Friedhof; to prune – beschneiden

"Come on then!"

By the afternoon we really were standing on the furthermost and southernmost point of the island. The beach was protected by gigantic black **chunks** of stone. Carlos said it was basalt. The wind blew strongly and wafted **surf** into our faces. I kissed Carlos. "Can you taste the salt on our lips? Your chin's salty, too," I remarked after I'd licked it briefly.

"Mimi!" Carlos cried in horror. "Are you turning into Noballs?"

Holly pointed out various birds and told us their names. But however much I tried, I found that they all looked the same.

"That's a **herring gull**! And that's a **sandpiper**! And look, there's an **oyster-catcher**!"

"Fine! You know what, Holly?" Carlos **bellowed** against the wind. "I'm cold! Can't we go somewhere to warm up?"

"To the *Malabar*!" she laughed.

My stomach was starting to rumble. "Hey, Holly, aren't you hungry?"

"Wait till we're in the *Malabar*, okay?"

So we got back on to our bikes and pedalled like mad. **Fate had it in for us**. We had a powerful head wind, and at one point I even got off because I thought I was about to be blown off my bike at any moment.

At last we reached the *Malabar*. There were so many cars in the car park that we could barely find

---

chunk – Brocken; surf – Gischt, Brandung; herring gull – Silbermöwe; sandpiper – Strandläufer; oyster-catcher – Austernfischer; to bellow – schreien; fate – Schicksal; to have it in for sb – jmdn. auf dem Kieker haben

space for our bikes. The pub – actually a huge hut, like in the Alps, only with huge windows and directly at the side of **or, rather**, almost on top of, the water – does, of course, have a fantastic view, and is totally 'in'. You could easily tell by the number of guests: they were sitting in, in front of, and even between the dunes.

First off, I buried my nose in the menu, ignoring the prices. Only when I'd **devoured** one of the house specials, curry sausage and chips, did I take in my surroundings.

And they really were worth seeing! All sorts of material for my stories was sitting here!

"Look, Mimi, that one at the next table is a TV presenter. The girl next to him is the one from 'Good Times, Bad Times' ..."

I couldn't get over it and made feverish notes on everything Holly said.

"What are you doing, Mimi? Are you writing postcards to your loved ones at home?"

I looked up. "Johanna!"

Johanna sat down with us without asking. "Constantin's not here yet?" she asked casually.

"If he's not at the table ...?" Carlos looked around **exaggeratedly**.

Johanna **shrugged her shoulders**. "So, Mimi, why are you writing? You're not from the press, are you?"

"No, no, she's practising her **calligraphy**," Carlos explained kindly.

---

or, rather – nein; to devour – verschlingen; exaggerated – übertrieben; to shrug your shoulders – mit den Schultern zucken; calligraphy – Handschrift

"Nonsense!" Johanna looked at my notebook without a trace of embarrassment. "You *are* from the press!"

"I'm far too young," I **deflected** her. "It's just as Carlos said, I'm practising my calligraphy."

Johanna didn't get the joke. She screwed up her nose, pulled a mirror out of her handbag and reapplied her lipstick, although hardly any of the colour had come off. "Tell me the truth: why are you writing down who all these people are? And what they look like?" she persisted.

Holly bent over the table and whispered **confidentially**, "She's still very young, but she's a genius, don't you know! She really is from the press; she's supposed to be writing all sorts of articles about what the island is famous for. Straight up, no joking! I've already shown her the unusual birds, and now we're here to –"

"So, what newspaper do you write for?" Johanna rudely interrupted her. "For the Sylt one?"

"Of course, for that one, too. But not just that one," Carlos assured her proudly, if not entirely truthfully.

I had to suppress a laugh because Johanna had **struck a pose** and suddenly turned **ingratiatingly** friendly. "I only gave you," she began, **coughing** discreetly, "incomplete information when we met at the pool. It's true that I'm doing my A' levels next year, but I'm already getting regular work with one of the 'in' modelling agencies. And I'm only on the

---

to deflect – ablenken, abbringen; confidential – vertraulich; to strike a pose – eine Pose einnehmen; ingratiating – einschmeichelnd; to cough – husten

island because my agent begged me to take part in this year's modelling competition. The event takes place at the weekend and my agent is convinced that I'll be the winner. Totally stressful, but it is, of course, important for the publicity, especially because my agent is building me up in a big way," she finished with a **sigh**.

"Is that true?" I asked Holly. "Is there really a modelling competition at the weekend?"

Holly nodded.

"Where? In Westerland?"

"At the airport. We've got a hall there for parties and special events like the modelling competition, for instance."

"Cool!" I made a note of the time and place. "Great subject for an article!"

Johanna coughed slightly again. "I'd be glad to co-operate with you. If it's okay by you, I'm available for interview. I don't think my agent will mind."

Now the three of us were shaken by a terrible coughing fit.

"Perhaps," gasped Carlos. "Perhaps your agent is also available? How about it, Johanna?"

"Good idea, Carlos," I praised him. "So who's your agent, Johanna? The one you jogged past on the beach? Or the one you were talking to in the pub in Kampen?"

Johanna shook her hair back in irritation. "**Neither**. He's not on Sylt at the moment."

"Oh, what a shame. Well, then I'll have a think about the interview idea," I said.

---

sigh – Seufzer; neither – weder noch

"Fine. I do, of course, mean an exclusive interview," said Johanna.

"Well, what else? I don't waste my time on **small fry**," I assured her casually. My God, this Johanna seemed pretty **dull-witted** and completely impervious to teasing.

But then it did turn into a fun evening after all. When Constantin appeared, she went into full-on chat-up mode, but after he'd shaken her hand off his arm for the third time, she got the message and left him in peace.

---

small fry – kleine Fische;
dull-witted – begriffsstutzig, blöd

Three Steps from Ruin!

The next morning Carlos and I were wandering hand-in-hand around Kampen. This early in the day, the village was dead; just two sleepy-looking people outside a café were staring **morosely** into their cups.

There wasn't much going on at the beach either. A couple of people were walking dogs on **leads**; others were jogging; others were just letting the wind **waft** around their noses.

It was a strong wind. It held our plastic bags containing our swimming things out completely horizontal, and although the waves crashed powerfully on the sand, we didn't feel much like swimming – I found it simply too cold for that. We pulled our shoes off, rolled our jeans up and walked right along the edge of the water in a northerly direction. After a few metres Carlos stopped and pointed to the **cliff** to our right. "I need to have a closer look at that," he murmured. "I'll be back in a second, okay?"

"Have you **spotted** a geological-geomorphological fault?" I cried after him, bending down to pick

---

morose – griesgrämig; lead – Leine; to waft – wehen, blasen; cliff – Klippe; to spot – erblicken, sehen

up a mussel. I didn't stop at one. I'd soon filled all my trouser pockets and had walked on so far that I'd lost sight of Carlos. So I turned round and discovered that the beach had in the meantime become pretty busy. The wind was blowing even more strongly, and I saw two boys raising first one then a second red ball on a mast. What did that mean? The boys looked fabulous: bronzed bodies, **ruffled** hair, blond **streaks**, broad grins, cool sunglasses; they had set up camp in a red hut on wheels. The bright yellow surfboard next to it looked good as well, and everything taken together – red hut, yellow board, blue waves, white **crests** – forced themselves upon me as a kitschy subject for a souvenir snapshot.

I sat on the sand, wrapping my arms around myself. Strange weather, I thought. Great sun – but this cold. Brr! The waves crashed on the sand. Two men were chatting near to me. The wind carried **snippets** of conversation over to me. "Stock market," I heard, along with "share price" and "Something-or-other Bank." Three children were playing peacefully in the sand with brightly coloured sandcastle **moulds**, little shovels and buckets. They probably belonged to the two men who were so animatedly discussing their finances.

"Hi, Mimi, I've found you at last!"

"Holly!"

"Great weather, isn't it?"

"Hey, aren't you freezing?"

"In this heat? You're **nuts**!"

---

ruffled – zerzaust; streak – Strähne; crest – Schaumkrone; snippet – Fetzen; mould – *hier:* Förmchen; to be nuts – verrückt sein

"Heat?" I scrutinized Holly's shorts and little shirt. "You're pretty hardy, aren't you? So what do those balls on the pole mean?"

"Absolutely no swimming," she explained briefly. "Stiff breeze, strong current and surf. Can you see those boys? They're our lifeguards. You know, like on Baywatch. It looks relaxed, but it's not a fun job. Where's Carlos?"

"Somewhere on the cliff," I explained.

"Why?" she asked, astonished.

"He's looking for a fault."

"You're pulling my leg!"

"No, honest! He's studying Geology, that's why."

"Why didn't he say so in the first place? I could tell him all kinds of things about the island ... Look, here comes Constantin!"

"All we need is Johanna," I grumbled. "But I can do without her."

"Me, too," said Holly, laughing. "Hi, Constantin, where have you left your constant companion?"

Constantin dropped down into the sand next to us. "No idea. I didn't choose her, but she sticks to me like chewing gum. My mother is pretty annoyed with her."

"Why?"

Constantin frowned. "She says she knows her type."

"Me, too. Carlos and I call them 'Wanda types'," I explained. "Johanna doesn't want to know Carlos, thankfully. He's too poor for her." We laughed.

Holly **dug** her toe into the sand. "Hey, Constantin, so what do you do?"

---

to dig – graben

"The same as you lot. I'm still at school. Year 12."

"What else? I mean, what do you do in your free time?" Holly persisted. "Tennis? Golf? Sailing? Parties? Do you have a job?"

"None of them." Constantin fell silent.

"Hey, tell us! School isn't everything, is it?"

"You wouldn't understand. You'd probably all laugh at me," he explained **reluctantly**. "Isn't anyone keeping an eye on those children?"

"Of course, they are. I think those two men are their fathers," I replied.

"Well, Constantin, aren't you **keeping us in suspense**." Holly put her head on one side. "Look, I'll take over our guest-house later on, so I'm already familiarizing myself with it. Mimi's going to be a journalist, Carlos is studying – what's he studying again?"

"Geology," I helped her out.

"That's it. He's studying Geology and is just examining that cliff behind us. And what do you do?"

"I'm interested in my computer, and apart from that, I read. I read a lot," Constantin finally explained.

"And you're ashamed of it? I don't get that."

I understood Constantin. Reading is something rather private, and if you tell people what you read, you're **revealing** something about yourself.

"And what do you read? Books about computers? Crime fiction?"

"See? You just think of the obvious things."

"Hey, don't **get worked up**!" Holly complained. "There's no crime in asking, is there?"

---

reluctant – widerwillig; to keep sb in suspense – jmdn. auf die Folter spannen; to reveal – aufdecken, verraten; to get worked up – sich aufregen

"No, but I don't have to answer!" Constantin kept on looking straight ahead. "Those fathers should keep a better eye on their children," he said under his breath. "They're playing too close to the water."

I couldn't really understand either why he didn't want to say what books he read, but Holly's curiosity was **a bit in your face**. Now she was leaning over to him and pulling at something yellow that was sticking out of his trouser pocket. I knew those little yellow books. School books! **Dreary** classics! Boring reading lessons! Sleeping lessons! I grinned.

"Hey! Leave it alone!" cried Constantin, slapping Holly's fingers.

But the yellow Reclam book was already lying in the sand. *Der Schimmelreiter,* I read. "Theodor Storm. – Are you reading that of your own free will?" I asked, astonished. "Well done!"

"If you write, you have to read as well," replied Constantin.

"Yes, but I'm interested in accounts of dangerous journeys and adventures."

Constantin nodded. "Something along the lines of 'just managed to escape again!', 'three steps from ruin!', or 'the water came up to my –'"

At that very moment someone dived above our heads. Sand sprayed in our eyes; we shouted, jumped up and – "Carlos!" I yelled.

I could just see him diving into the waves, fully clothed, his arms outstretched as he took a gigantic leap. Then he disappeared.

"Carlos!"

---

to be a bit in sb's face – penetrant sein, offensichtlich sein; dreary – eintönig, langweilig

His head emerged from the water for a fraction of a second.

The two Baywatchers who had **hoisted up** the red balls sprinted past us and threw themselves likewise into the waves.

"What's happened?" asked a fat woman.

"I think one of the children ..."

"Sandra!" yelled one of the **stocks-and-shares** men. "My God, Sandra!" He pulled off his shoes and ran across the beach in his socks.

"Stay here! Don't you go into the water, too!" the other man yelled, holding him back.

A wave threw the little red plastic bucket up on to the beach.

But where was Carlos?

I was terrified for him. If the current had grabbed him, if he'd been carried out into the open sea, if – and this on such a **packed**, even lifeguarded, beach of all beaches!

But there he was! Carlos emerged, followed shortly by the others.

"Who does the girl belong to?" asked Carlos.

"She's mine!" The father was completely beside himself.

"She's fine," said one of the boys who'd plunged into the water as well. "But I can't understand why you weren't keeping a better eye on your child. You can see the red balls, for goodness' sake! Absolutely no swimming!"

"Yes, of course, but ... I just don't know how it happened! Sandra, are you okay?"

---

to hoist up – hissen; stocks and shares – Aktien; packed – gerammelt voll mit Menschen

"She just wanted to fetch some water! To bake sand cakes!" wailed one of the children.

I clung to the **dripping** Carlos.

Holly took the sobbing little boy in her arms and comforted him. "It's over, calm down. Sandra's fine, she just had quite a **fright**."

---

dripping – tropfend; fright – Schreck

Carlos is a hero!

The fathers and the coastguard boys exchanged addresses. "But *he* was in fact the one who noticed first," one of them said, pointing to Carlos. "What's your name?" "That's got nothing to do with anything," said Carlos. "I just happened to see the little one being caught up by the wave, and dived in after her. Anyone would have done the same."

"He's called Carlos, and he's staying at Lornsen's at the moment," Holly declared unasked. "You'll find the address in the telephone book."

There was a bit more **to-ing and fro-ing**, someone fetched a blanket and wrapped the sobbing Sandra up in it, then the fathers tramped off with their children. They left behind the little moulds for making sand cakes and the washed-up little red bucket.

The crowd **dispersed**.

"**Blimey**," one of the Baywatch boys said to Carlos. "We've **had our fingers crossed** all morning, hoping that nothing would happen. We were look-

---

hero – Held; to-ing and fro-ing – Hin und Her;
to disperse – zerstreuen; Blimey! – Verdammt!;
to have your fingers crossed – die Daumen drücken

ing everywhere – and then this happens! It was brilliant, the way you did that."

"What was it again?" I realized that my teeth were still chattering. "Real adventures happen in the mind? It's not true. Carlos, what if you had **drowned**!"

"But I didn't. It really wasn't dangerous. You could just as easily have pulled that child out of the water if you'd seen her."

"But we didn't see her, even though we were sitting right in front of her," said Constantin. "Mimi, do you remember? We were talking about true adventures. 'Three steps from ruin!' and 'just managed to escape again!' But this here was real life, not literature!"

"Carlos, you have to take those wet clothes off!" commanded Holly.

Carlos jumped up. "You're right. This wind is damned cold." He set off with his plastic bag in the direction of the dunes, and returned with his swimming trunks on and a towel **wrapped round** him.

"Carlos, you're a hero," said Holly. "You'll be in the Sylt papers tomorrow."

"Nonsense. – I need to put something warm on. Are you coming, Mimi?"

No way would I have let him go on his own.

"I'll go with them," Holly said to Constantin. "What are your plans?"

"In exactly –" he looked at his watch, "in exactly 21 minutes I'm meeting my mother for lunch in the *Village Pitcher*."

---

to drown – ertrinken; to wrap round – herumwickeln; no way – auf keinen Fall

"Okay. Then we'll see each other again," declared Holly.

"You really enjoy organizing other people's lives, don't you?" asked Constantin.

Holly **stopped short**. "Do I do that?"

"You certainly do – you never stop," replied Constantin. "Haven't you noticed?"

"Nah." Holly swallowed. "I – er – I don't **mean any harm**."

Constantin looked at her thoughtfully. "True. It's probably just the way you are."

Holly turned bright red. "Fine, then let's not bother."

"What do you mean?"

"Then we won't meet up with you later, when Carlos has got changed, you **donkey**."

Now it was Constantin's turn to go red. "Whatever!"

"Just stop **quarrelling**, we're off," I said, taking Carlos' arm. "See you, then!"

Neither of them took any notice of us.

Märthe was standing in the open door. "I already know everything! Someone from the Sylt paper was just on the phone. He wanted to know if you were back home yet, Carlos. I said you'd be back in ten minutes. The ten minutes are up now."

"Märthe!"

The telephone rang and Carlos raced off.

"I told him we had a **resident** expert here," Märthe explained further. "He said that was great

---

to stop short – plötzlich stehen bleiben;
to mean any harm – es böse meinen; donkey – Esel;
to quarrel – streiten; resident – ansässig

and that he'd like to meet you sometime as well, Mimi. He'll probably come for tea this afternoon. **At any rate**, I told him the cake would be ready by tea-time and that he was very welcome to come."

"Märthe, you're impossible!"

"That's what Albrecht Lornsen always says," she said, unfazed.

"Where is Albrecht?"

"He's taking Noballs for a walk. Come on into the kitchen. I've boiled some water; the boy needs a hot drink."

"Okay ...," we could hear him saying. "If that's the way it has to be ... You've already discussed it with Märthe? ... Well, then! ... At tea-time ... Yes. Bye."

"Well, what did I say?! He's coming at tea-time." Märthe handed Carlos a glass. "Take care. It's hot!"

"Blimey, Märthe, it's just so embarrassing," wailed Carlos.

"What is? The fact that you saved a child from drowning? I know people who'd find it embarrassing if they *hadn't* saved a child from drowning," she **retorted** indignantly.

You couldn't discuss anything with Märthe; she just talked you into the ground and always had the last word.

The whole house was **snug** and comfortable, but the most comfortable place of all was the kitchen. We were sitting at the table. Märthe had forced the grog upon the protesting Carlos, saying, "So you want to **keep your trap shut**? We've got our own

---

at any rate – auf jeden Fall; to retort – scharf erwidern; snug – behaglich; to keep your trap shut – seinen Mund halten

medicine for that on this island!" And now we were spooning up a hot soup. Potato soup, naturally!

We chatted away and listened to Märthe's stories. We found out the difference between pirates and **wreckers**, and in the process discovered that the wall tiles in the front room, the 'Piisel', weren't fixed on as a precaution against high water, but that this custom came from the merchants who brought them back as desirable **mementoes** of their voyages.

"I've even got a **shrunken head** at home," Märthe declared proudly. "Belonging to my great-great-grandfather."

"What? Your great-great-grandfather's shrunken head?" I couldn't believe it. "Who on earth went to the trouble of preserving his head? Isn't that completely **disgusting**?"

"Why's it disgusting? For one thing, it's not his own head, but one that he brought back from Borneo with him; and for another, it's only supposed to be a monkey's head. All the same, it's a treasure."

When the doorbell rang, we jumped. "The press?"

But it was Holly, who was bringing an invitation from Constantin's mother. "We can't, the guy from the Sylt paper is coming later," we said **regretfully**.

"But he's only coming for tea," said Märthe. "Couldn't you make it later? Give her a call, Holly."

Carlos and I shook our heads. Organizing was evidently one of the islanders' favourite **pursuits**.

Holly immediately ran to the telephone and then told us, grinning, that Constantin's mother had in-

---

wrecker – Strandräuber; memento – Andenken; shrunken head – Schrumpfkopf; disgusting – ekelhaft; regretful – bedauernd; pursuit – Beschäftigung

stantly invited us for 'after tea'. "At her hotel. She's sending a taxi."

"Because you're famous," Märthe remarked.

Later on, however, it **transpired** that Märthe's **suspicions** had been completely wrong. The reason for the invitation was so unusual that – but I'll tell you everything when we get to that point.

In any case, Jens-Uwe from the Sylt paper arrived shortly after Holly's phone call. It took Carlos half a minute to tell him what he saw and did, and that the whole thing wasn't **remotely** a question of courage.

Jens-Uwe wrote everything down dutifully and then said, "Well, it's not the first time a child's been rescued on Sylt, is it?"

He banged Carlos on the shoulder. "The **peculiar** thing about this case is your **modesty**. You should have heard the **fuss** the guy made who pulled a dog out of the water!" He turned to me. "And so you want to become one of my colleagues?" he asked from on high. "Let me know when you make it, okay? Till then!"

I hate people who treat me as if I were still a child. "I'll be sending him copies of our *Daily Post*," I said through **gritted** teeth. "When you make it! Ha! The only thing he's got over me is age!"

"And a **pinch** of experience," added Märthe **matter-of-factly**. "But I do think he could have been nicer to you!"

---

to transpire – durchsickern; suspicion – Verdacht;
not remotely – nicht im Entferntesten;
peculiar – besonders; modesty – Bescheidenheit;
fuss – Wirbel, Getue; gritted – zusammengebissen;
pinch – Prise; matter-of-factly – sachlich, nüchtern

The invitation

We hadn't seen anything of Johanna for the whole day. "I wonder whether she's been invited, too?" I asked Holly.

She shook her head firmly. "Don't think so. You see, I heard Constantin's mother saying to him, 'And make sure that this Johanna doesn't hear about the invitation. I don't want her here.'"

"I don't get it," said Carlos. "There's something going on that we don't know anything about."

"Then let's be surprised," I said. "I like surprises, especially when they don't **concern** me!"

"Who knows ..." Carlos smiled quietly to himself.

Märthe **scurried** around us, making sure that we dressed up as smartly as possible. "You **owe** it to the lady," she assured us earnestly. "If she's staying in *Behind the Dunes*, she'll expect it of you. Do you even know what she's called?"

"No idea. We just know Constantin."

She sighed. "If only I knew where Albrecht Lornsen had got to. But he never tells me when he'll

---

to concern – betreffen; to scurry – hasten, huschen; to owe – schulden be back! Today of all days, when we need him, he disappears."

"We thought that, too, when we arrived here."

"He was always a **loner** and has never – listen! That's your taxi!"

A moment later, we were getting into the car.

"To the hotel *Behind the Dunes* in Keitum," said Holly, taking the front seat next to the driver. "Oh, it's you, hello, Björn! **Put your foot down** a bit and do us a special price, okay?"

"Holly! Slowly, slowly! Always **flat-out**, aren't you?"

Holly laughed and turned to us in the back. "Björn is our neighbour. We've known one another since forever."

Carlos and I held hands for the whole of the journey. If I had lost Carlos – unthinkable! Funny, the way that particular events really show you how much you like someone. Is that why terrible things happen?! I took my new notebook out of the plastic bag and made a note of that thought.

When you drive up to a hotel in a taxi, you get a completely different perspective from when you're pedalling along on a vintage bike and fighting with a head wind **to boot**. We got out, marched up to reception, and were shown into a small tea-room: tiled walls of course – they had to be –, and a view of the park. Constantin was already hurrying towards us.

---

loner – Einzelgänger; to put one's foot down – aufs Gas treten; flat-out – geradeheraus; to boot – obendrein, noch dazu

"All it needs is for him to take us in his arms and give us little kisses," I teased under my breath.

"Pull yourself together, Mimi," whispered Carlos.

"Why? Nobody here knows me."

"True. But I know you well enough to know that you're capable of anything. Just you remember the red card."

I giggled. "Look!" I pulled the yellow card out of my trouser pocket.

Carlos shut his eyes in horror. "Real adventures happen in the mind, Mimi. Oh God, but there isn't any adventure here."

"Only on the beach," I reassured him.

"Could you two please stop that whispering?" **hissed** Holly. "Behave yourselves, got it?"

Constantin spared us the outstretched arms and kisses on the cheek. "Mimi, Holly, Carlos," he introduced us. "This is my mother. Frau Rieck."

"My name is Susanne," said Frau Rieck, shaking our hands. "I don't imagine you want tea now. Juice? Cola? What would you like?"

We agreed on cola and **lapsed** into an uncomfortable silence. Frau Rieck was a fantastically beautiful woman, but a pinch of Holly's spirit wouldn't have done her any harm. She seemed so ... tired? Yes, that was it. I remembered that her husband had only died a couple of months before. That was presumably the reason why she looked so tired. I'd have liked to give her a large portion of **joie de vivre**, if only I could. And I noticed something else. She brushed her hair off her forehead with a partic-

---

to hiss – zischen, fauchen; to lapse – verfallen;
joie de vivre – Lebensfreude

ularly elegant hand movement. Constantin had this habit, too. He pushed his hair back just like his mother.

"You were no doubt surprised by the invitation," she began. "It's just that I like to get to know Constantin's friends. Especially when they're such unusual people as you."

That was **laid on pretty thick**. I cleared my throat and **trod surreptitiously** on Carlos' foot.

Carlos, of course, had to recount the story of his bold rescue of the child, and Holly had to talk about her guest-house. "How old is the house?" enquired Frau Rieck.

"Built in 1778," Holly replied promptly. "It's still got all its original features ... well, almost original," she qualified.

"I came to the island for the first time exactly 25 years ago," said Frau Rieck

"To our guest-house?" asked Holly immediately.

"No, to a children's home. I worked as a '**maid of all work**' during the vacations. It was a fantastic time for me."

"Tell us!" I demanded, secretly showing Carlos a corner of my yellow card. "Did you have some real adventures?"

"That depends on what you mean by 'real adventures'. At any rate, I didn't rescue any children, but just enjoyed my life. You know, I had what they call a '**sheltered upbringing**', and the time on Sylt was my first holiday without my parents."

---

to lay on pretty thick – ziemlich dick auftragen; to trod – treten; surreptitious – heimlich; maid of all work – Mädchen für alles; sheltered upbringing – behütete Kindheit

"Did something particular happen?" I asked, in order to get her back on the subject. After all, I needed material for my article, and I could suddenly sense a story here. "I mean, just for our information."

She told us this and that, and how at the end of that October a real **storm tide** broke out over the island, and she had got what was called **'Island Rage'**. "I just wanted to leave," she recalled. "I wanted to go somewhere where I didn't need a ship or a plane or a train just to get from A to B. I suddenly felt like a prisoner."

We nodded. "Yes, of course, I can understand that," said Holly. "Some guests do feel like that when things get tight. When they think that something's trying to **hem** them **in**."

Frau Rieck stopped short. "Come to think of it, that was my second dose of Island Rage," she said thoughtfully.

"What about the first?" I **probed**. I felt like Holly on the morning she'd been interrogating Constantin. But if there wasn't a story in the air, then my name wasn't Mimi Muschalek!

Frau Rieck suddenly looked like a young girl. "I've never told anyone this story," she said, and we noticed how undecided she still was.

"Come on, Mum, don't be a **spoil-sport**!" Constantin now begged her. "What does it matter? It's all so long ago. All gone and forgotten."

"Oh? Is it?" She frowned. "All right then. Here is

---

storm tide – Sturmflut; Island Rage – Inselkoller;
to hem in – einengen; to probe – nachforschen;
spoil-sport – Spielverderber

the story. I turned 20 while I was on Sylt," she began. "I had decided to celebrate this birthday in a quite special way."

"And how was that?" I asked, thrilled.

"Like in a fairy-tale. I had three wishes. Three wishes that were linked to one another. I wanted to be invited to a casino on my 20th birthday – as I told you, I had a protected childhood. I wanted someone to **propose** to me – it wouldn't have been my first proposal, but I thought my birthday would be a suitable opportunity for another. And I wanted someone to give me 20 **long-stemmed** roses – that seemed to me to be more harmless than a diamond ring."

"Ugh!" Holly giggled. "Well, you were a modest one. Did you even have a boyfriend?"

"Several," replied Frau Rieck coolly. "That wasn't the problem. The problem was that I didn't want to marry any of them. I wanted to finish studying as quickly as possible, earn my own money and be absolutely free."

"Then I don't understand the three wishes," I said. "You could have wished for something completely different, couldn't you? Nobody forced you to make those wishes."

"No, nobody. I still don't know to this day which little high-spirited devil whispered them into my ear. But there they were, and I was **determined** to **fulfil** them. Among my friends on the island there was a man who ... who had an interesting job and

---

to propose – *hier:* einen Heiratsantrag machen; long-stemmed – langstielig; to be determined – entschlossen sein; to fulfil – erfüllen

stood on his own two feet. He was much older than me, you know. This very man invited me for a drink in Kampen one evening. 'It's your birthday in three days', he said. I hadn't told him anything about it, so I wanted to know how he knew the date. 'Professional secret', he replied. 'I'd like to celebrate the day with you.' But he couldn't because I had to work. So we agreed that he'd pick me up at eight o'clock in the evening. He didn't ask what I wanted; he didn't ask how I in fact wanted to celebrate – he didn't ask anything. But that evening he was standing outside the house. First of all we went for a lovely and very expensive meal, then we played several rounds in the casino, and finally he pressed into my arms 20 of the longest-stemmed roses I'd ever seen, and asked me if I'd marry him."

"Who did you tell about the three wishes?" I asked, thrilled.

"Not a **soul**," she **assured** me. "Really, not a single soul. I thought myself that the three wishes were as ridiculous as anything."

We looked at her **disbelievingly**.

"So he guessed them himself?" Holly asked uncertainly.

"He must have done."

"What ... what did you say to him?" I asked.

She laughed. "Exactly what any girl would have said in my position: thank you, I'll think about it."

"That was a clear no," said Carlos.

She nodded. "Correct. I didn't love him; I was just playing with him."

---

soul – Seele; to assure – versichern;
disbelieving – ungläubig

"What about him?" I asked further.

"I only met him one more time. The next day. And never again."

"Wow!" That was Holly.

I swallowed. "Do you know anything about him?"

She hesitated. "Maybe. I'm not sure. I only know that he never married."

"What a story!" I pulled the yellow card out of my trouser pocket and held it out to her.

"Real adventures happen in the mind," she read aloud. She turned red. "True." She brushed her hair off her forehead again, and abruptly changed the subject. "So? What else have you got on your **schedule** for today?"

"The *Malabar*," Holly answered promptly.

"Well, then off you go!"

In the taxi – she had got us a taxi again – I whispered in Carlos' ear, "She was a real Wanda, don't you reckon?"

"Yes ... she was. But she isn't any more."

"True. She's changed." I fell silent, lost in thought. "Something changed her. But what?"

"No idea. We're here already. Everyone out."

The pub was packed. We pushed our way through the people, searching for an empty seat.

"Help!" Constantin held us back. "Johanna's sitting over there."

As bad luck would have it – or, as it turned out, good luck – there was just one table left, and it was the one Johanna had her back to.

We **sneaked in** – and couldn't believe our ears.

---

schedule – Plan; to sneak in – hineinschleichen

"… model," Johanna was saying. She had to talk very loudly because of the noise. "Of course, my boyfriend doesn't like to see it at all. He's so jealous! By the way, I'm giving an exclusive interview to Mimi, a top journalist who just happens to be staying on the island. She was most **insistent** and said she'd probably not get the chance once I'd won first prize in the show. What else could I do?"

"Of course," said the guy next to her. "If you're desirable and kind-hearted, it's just one **obligation** after the next. I know how it is. I …"

We looked at one another, dumbfounded. "The *Malabar* isn't the in place for us today," I hissed. "Come on, let's get out of here! We'll find another pub!"

---

insistent – hartnäckig; obligation – Verpflichtung

Rivals on the scene

I could hear **crockery** banging and could smell freshly-brewed coffee. Mmmm ... With one **bound** I jumped out of bed, banged my head on the beams as always, and shortly afterwards ran downstairs to Märthe in the kitchen.

"Morning! Sleep well?" she pointed to the Sylt paper.

"Yes ... Wow, what a big article! And a picture, too! I don't get it!"

"I've made waffles to celebrate," Märthe declared proudly. "My speciality!"

I read. "Thanks to the brave actions of a young man, a child was saved from drowning yesterday. At the time of the accident there was a stiff south-westerly breeze with a strong current; the lifeguards had raised up two red balls which, as everyone knows, means absolutely no swimming. **Nevertheless** – " I looked up. "Crikey, Märthe, where's Carlos? Is he still **kipping**? And Albrecht? How can anyone sleep when they're featured in such a big way in the papers? The pair of them absolutely have to –"

---

crockery – Geschirr; bound – Sprung; caution – Vorsicht; nevertheless – wie auch immer; to kip – schlafen

The doorbell rang like mad. "The press?"

"The neighbours, more likely," **conjectured** Märthe, going to the door. "Holly! Come in!"

"Have you already seen it? – Yes you have, there's the paper. Great, eh? Where's Carlos?"

"He's still asleep."

Holly shook her head in disbelief. "Does he want to turn into a **log**?"

"No, I think I'll stick to being human," said Carlos as he came running down the stairs. "What's this all about?"

"About you," Holly answered promptly. "Carlos, there's a huge feature on you in the papers! How can you sleep?"

"Show me ..." He **plonked himself down** on the first chair he could find, and pulled the newspaper towards him.

"Hey, what about my good-morning kiss?" I was really annoyed. "Only just famous, and you're already writing me off. I hadn't thought that of you, Carlos."

"In a minute ... My God, haven't they **laid it on**!"

"But it's all true, isn't it?" Holly devoured one waffle after another. The doorbell rang again.

"Press?" asked Holly, chewing.

"The neighbours, more likely," Märthe and I replied simultaneously.

Again, it wasn't the neighbours.

"I'm sorry to disturb you so early, but could I have a word with Mimi and Carlos, please?"

---

to conjecture – vermuten; log – Holzklotz;
to plonk oneself down – sich hinschmeißen;
to lay it on – übertreiben

"Constantin! What are you doing here? Did you come by taxi?" Holly asked immediately.

"On my bike," he said, taken aback. "You're here, too!"

"Yes, as you can see," Holly retorted **cuttingly**. "Is that a problem?"

"What the devil's going on here? Yesterday I had an orderly house, but today it's like Piccadilly Circus." Albrecht shuffled into the kitchen. "My God, Märthe, have you taken in new lodgers? The house is much too small."

"Albrecht! You're talking before you've had your third cup of coffee! Why's that?"

"I'd like to know, too ... why's the paper on the middle of the table? Ah, now I'm beginning to understand. It's because of the article about the brave life-saver." With a practised grip he seized the newspaper and put his reading glasses on. "**Misplaced** comma in the third line ... Unnecessary exclamation mark in the sixth ... New paragraph after the tenth is missing ... oh well, that aside, it's not a bad article. Märthe, where's my coffee got to?"

"It's next to you," I said, pushing the cup nearer.

"Thank you. Oh, you're here, too, Holly. Nice to see you. How's your grandfather?"

"He's still on Amrum. The funeral seems to be going on and on."

Albrecht grinned. "You have to celebrate parties as they happen. So, and who are you?" he asked Constantin.

"He's one of our friends," I explained quickly.

---

cutting – schneidend;
to be misplaced – an der falschen Stelle sein

"We got to know him **by chance**. He reads a lot, Albrecht."

"So. He reads a lot. Has the reader got a name?"

"Good morning, Herr Lornsen. My name is Constantin and I'm staying with my mother in Keitum at the moment." Constantin really did have simply fabulous manners. My aunts would have loved the boy!

"Hmm. In Keitum. Where?"

"In *Behind the Dunes*," replied Holly. "His mother invited us there yesterday."

"Why? She presumably wanted to know what kind of people her son hangs around with?"

We laughed. "She said something along those lines," Constantin said, embarrassed, and brushed his hair off his forehead.

Albrecht stopped short. He scrutinized Constantin closely. "Do that again," he said abruptly.

"Sorry? What do you want me to do?"

"Brush your hair away from your forehead again, okay?"

Constantin turned red.

"Albrecht!" cried Märthe. "Is that a way to treat your guest?!"

"I'm probably not quite awake yet," he said **gruffly**. "Is there any more coffee?"

An uncomfortable silence **ensued**. Even Holly, self-confident as she was, was lost for words. Albrecht slurped his coffee noisily, Märthe was busy with the waffle iron, and I was cross because Carlos still hadn't given me my good-morning kiss.

Albrecht put down his cup. "So. I'm done," he

---

by chance – zufällig; gruff – schroff; to ensue – folgen

declared. "Mimi and Carlos, I'll show you the Red Cliff today, along with the Uwe-Dune and the List Wanderdünen."

"What?" Holly sprang up. "That's my job, Albrecht!" she cried. "That's precisely why I'm here!"

I hate it when people go over my head and plan the day for me. I hate it even more when Carlos, without having spoken to me, accepts offers that interest me either **barely** or not at all. "Why don't we all go together?" he suggested.

"I'm interested in people!" I snapped.

"But you have to see the Uwe-Dune," Albrecht said energetically. "Then you can worry about people."

"Look, Albrecht," Holly tapped the picture in the newspaper, "these are quite special guests, so I'll look after them especially well. Okay?"

"My goodness, girl, you really are **getting stuck in**!" Albrecht laughed suddenly. "Okay, I get the message. So, what do you want to do today?"

"I thought ..." Holly began, but I interrupted her. "I'll go with you, if I absolutely have to, to the Uwe-Dune, and then I'll bike over to Maike in *Behind the Dunes*. After all, I'm not on the island to enjoy myself; I've got to get material for my stories."

There was a bit more to-ing and fro-ing because Constantin immediately said he wanted to go to Keitum with me. That made Carlos **prick up his ears**. He declared that he'd come along an hour later and meet me in Keitum.

---

barely – kaum; to get stuck in – sich ins Zeug legen; to prick up one's ears – die Ohren spitzen

"We can't do that," Holly protested. "We need a full day for the dunes and stuff!"

Carlos hesitated. I could, on the one hand, see exactly how **tempting** the geological-geomorphological faults were, but how on the other, he didn't entirely trust Constantin, and would prefer not to let me out of his sight.

"We don't always have to stick together like two pieces of chewing gum with all the juice sucked out of them, Carlos," I said finally. "We'll meet up again this evening, okay?"

"And you don't mind me taking over your job, Albrecht?" Holly wanted to make sure.

"That entirely depends. If you're **doing him a favour**, then no. But if you've got some kind of nonsense in mind, then ..."

Holly turned red. So she *had* got nonsense in mind! I could just imagine why she was fighting to take over as tour-guide and spend the day with Carlos. Oh well, that was her problem. After the Wanda business, Carlos would know how to deal with Holly.

I quickly fetched my notebook and anorak, and then we began our tour.

We cycled from our Sjipwai – which, as we had discovered from Märthe, meant 'Sheep's Path' – into the centre of the village and turned into a little street that was in fact called 'To the Uwe-Dune'. After a few minutes we were fighting our way through the sand, then we found ourselves standing at the foot of the island's highest elevation: the mountain **loomed** a good 52 metres up into the

---

tempting – verführerisch; to do sb a favour – jmdm. einen Gefallen tun; to loom – aufragen

sky. Like a real **summit** in the mountains, it also has its own name. Not Zugspitze or Feldberg, obviously; these names are already taken. It's called Uwe. Plain and simple: Uwe.

A broad wooden staircase led to the summit, and there was a little platform with little benches to rest on every 18 steps, in order to stop people from overdoing it energy-wise. The last eleven steps led us to the largest and topmost platform, and if I'd thought the view wouldn't be worth the 52-metre climb, I had been very wrong. You really could see all sorts of things from up here: the water on one side, the dunes on the other side and straight ahead, and the straw-covered roofs of Kampen on the remaining side.

There were eight information boards, but we couldn't get to them because of the crush of visitors, so Holly really got stuck in. "So, the dune is named Uwe after one of our freedom fighters who **spurred on** our men 150 years ago in battle against Denmark. But you're not interested in history, are you? Fine. The island is exactly 35 kilometres long, and the bit we're standing on now is the very heart of the island, which consists of **moraine** material from the last Ice Age but one ..." Holly knew her stuff, that much was clear. But the little boy who'd just **thrust** his fist in front of his mother's nose and was earnestly asking her, "I've caught a mosquito, Mummy. Should I **squash** it or let it go?" was, to my mind, far more interesting.

---

summit – Gipfel; to spur on – anspornen;
moraine – Moräne, Gletschergeröll;
to thrust – stoßen; to squash – zerquetschen

His mother answered coolly, "Do you know if there's a vet around here? No? Then you'd better let it go unharmed."

Constantin burst out, "Classy sort, eh?"

I pointed with my chin at Carlos and Holly. "Come on, let's leave them to their faults."

We waited until Holly finally inserted a pause. "... Everyone knows that you could get from here to England on foot 10,000 years ago. Then, the Thames was just a **tributary** of the Rhine."

"Get that! Are you pulling our legs, or is that true?" I asked disbelievingly.

"It's true. Harpoon tips made of bone that have been washed up from the **depths** of the sea prove it," Holly defended her point.

I wrote it in my notebook just to be on the safe side, so that I could check it out later, then I said, "So, we're going to **beat it** now, okay? See you this evening. Bye!"

Constantin and I jumped down the steps and pedalled off, with a head-wind and accompanied by occasional rain-showers. Typical island weather, then. It suited me. I was a bit cross with Carlos. No kiss, no goodbye, not a kind word!

The only thing he was interested in was the dunes, cliffs and Holly's information. And she, single-minded and energetic as she was, was evidently after Carlos. Hopefully Carlos wouldn't start to weaken. I could bear *one* Wanda. A second one, even if she were called Holly, would be precisely one too many.

---

tributary – Nebenfluss; depth – Tiefe; to beat it – abhauen

A wicker beach chair in the evening sun

We found Maike on the patio, where she was drying off the tables and chairs after the last rain shower.

"Oh, so you're the girl who wants some good hotel stories? Sorry, but I can't help. All I can tell you about is the **groping** men and the men who come here with their girlfriends, and then swap rooms when their wives appear. Dreary stories, I can tell you."

Disappointed, I put my notebook away.

"Hi!"

"Johanna! What are you doing here?"

"Constantin!" She put her arms around his neck. "I've been looking for you everywhere," she **trilled**, kissing him on the cheek.

Was that embarrassing to him or what?

"Why?"

Johanna, who looked **enviably** good in her white jeans, handed him an envelope. "I wanted to give you the invitation in person. You're coming, aren't you?"

---

to grope – fummeln; to trill – trällern;
enviable – beneidenswert

She turned to me. "You, too, Mimi. Please don't disappoint me."

"So what's it all about?" I asked.

"I don't believe it! I hope you haven't forgotten the big event the modelling show at the weekend. In the party hall at Westerland Airport. There's not a better location on the island. All the important people will be there. And please, Mimi, you're going to write an article about me, aren't you? I'm really counting on it!"

"Oh God ..."

"I'm in a rush at the moment," Johanna **prattled on**. "See you! On Saturday at the latest, okay? I've found someone to drive me out here, and I can't keep him waiting too long."

We stared after her, speechless.

"Who on earth was that?" asked Maike.

"She's called Johanna ... Says she's a model," I answered **forcedly**.

"She creates quite a **stir**, doesn't she?" commented Constantin.

"Where does she live? I only ask because her address will tell you quite a lot," said Maike.

Constantin and I looked at one another. Neither of us knew.

"Then she can't have got all that far," said Maike. "She's probably staying in a third-class guest-house. Would you like to see a particularly nice room, Mimi?"

It wasn't a room: it was what's known as a 'suite', so a real apartment. All in all, it wasn't exactly

---

to prattle on – plappern; forced – gezwungen;
stir – Aufruhr

small, and was much smarter than what I was used to at home. I swallowed. "Bit more comfortable than in a tent, isn't it?"

Constantin, shy Constantin, put his arm around me, "Wow, Mimi! You're fantastic. I like you!"

That's all I needed, I thought. When I already had enough trouble with Carlos!

I thanked Maike and did what people always do in embarrassing situations: I looked **studiedly** at the time, cried, "Crikey, look how late it is!" and said goodbye in no time at all.

Carlos was sitting on the bench outside Albrecht's house. "Are you by any chance waiting for me?" I asked.

"Nah, for the first **bat** to come out," he replied grumpily. "You were gone for ages, Mimi."

"So?"

"Yes."

We didn't speak to one another until Carlos resumed the conversation.

"Albrecht said it was always quite interesting in the *Windhaube* in the evening. Live music and lots of people. He said we couldn't leave the island without having been there."

"Oh!"

"Yes. Should we ... I mean, do you fancy going to the *Windhaube*?"

"Don't know. How would we get there?"

"On the bikes."

"What? Did we book a cycling holiday? I bet we'd have a head wind the whole way."

---

studied – beabsichtigt; bat – Fledermaus

Fortunately, I still had the notebook in my bag, and was already wearing my anorak. So off we pedalled in a northerly direction, diagonally across the dunes. It wasn't far, and the head wind stayed within manageable proportions; and the fact that we even managed to grab some unoccupied wicker chairs wasn't bad either. I pulled my notebook out of my bag, put it on the table, and screwed up my eyes because the sun was blinding me. It was already pretty low down, and we could hear the **faint** sound of the waves running onto the beach.

"What did you two get up to today?" Carlos asked **presently**.

"We?" I frowned. "We?"

"You and Constantin."

"Well ... what did we do ... Well, first we were up on that Dieter-Dune –"

"Uwe-Dune."

I grinned. "Up on the dune. Then we cycled to Keitum, met Maike, then Johanna arrived with an invitation to the big modelling show on Saturday. That was it. And what did Holly show you?"

"The Red Cliff and the Wanderdünen in the north of the island."

"What are Wanderdünen?"

"Sand that the wind blows from the west to the east," Carlos explained curtly.

"Busy guy, that wind." I stole a look at Carlos.

"Mimi, why didn't you stay with me?"

"Why didn't you come with me?"

We flashed our eyes at one another.

Carlos swallowed heavily. "Look, Mimi, you met

---

faint – schwach; presently – bald danach

that Jonny in the Abruzzi; here, the guy in the pub tries to get off with you; and if you think I don't know that Constantin wanted to spend the whole day alone with you, you must think I'm pretty stupid."

"Oh!" I was pretty angry. "And I have to remind you of Wanda, unfortunately. And what's going on with Holly? Well?"

Instead of counter-attacking, Carlos merely said, "I know. She said she was in love with me."

That completely took the wind out of my sails.

"What about you? Are you in love with her, too?" I asked in horror.

"Course not. But what about you and Constantin? Have you fallen for him?"

"Carlos! How stupid can you be?!"

"Honestly? I was so afraid ..."

We kissed. When we'd finished kissing, it wasn't only all the trouble that had disappeared, but the sun, too.

Island stories

= - = - = - = - = - =

The next morning we were still sitting in the kitchen with Albrecht and Märthe when Holly was yet again standing on the doormat.

"Hi! My grandfather got back yesterday. He's expecting you, Mimi."

I looked at her in surprise. "He's always on particularly good form in the morning," Holly explained breathlessly. "It's the best time to get him to tell you his stories."

"Okay, then. Carlos, are you coming with me?"

"He can't. I want to show him Morsum Cliff. We arranged it yesterday, didn't we, Carlos?"

"Yes. B-but," he stammered.

"Mimi! He absolutely has to see the cliff! It's one of the most important geological monuments in the whole of Germany! The **mica** contains fossils that are between five and seven million years old!"

"It is as Holly says," Albrecht joined in. "The white sand got through Scandinavian rivers into the Sylt area. It contains **fossilized** sea lilies, corals and **sponges**, and the fossils look so strange that

---

mica – Glimmer (Mineralgruppe); fossilized – versteinert; sponge – Schwamm

the Sylt people say they are **remnants** of the 'Underworld'. No question about it, as a budding geologist, Carlos absolutely has to see the cliff, Mimi!"

"Precisely! That's just what I said!" Holly added quickly.

"Why don't the three of you go?" Märthe wanted to know.

That was exactly what I had just been about to suggest, but Holly beat me to it. "Oh, Märthe, Mimi's not interested in that. Carlos said so, too, didn't he? In any case, my grandfather's waiting for her."

I hesitated. Holly had worked that one very nicely. She sent me off to her grandfather according to the motto: this is what you wanted, so get on with it. And she was **luring** my Carlos **away** with geological sensations. Holly was ingenious and crafty, but the question was: what would Carlos choose?

"How long would we need, Holly?" he asked.

"Three hours," replied Albrecht.

"Four, more like. Or even five. It depends." Holly corrected him.

It depends? What did she mean by that? In any case, instead of saying, Listen, Holly, Mimi and I are sticking together. We'll visit your grandfather first, then cycle to the cliff, and that's that! Carlos shuffled uncomfortably around on his chair.

I pricked up my ears.

"Look, Mimi ..." he began.

That was enough. "Fine. Have fun at the cliff. And with Wanda Number Two," I added **maliciously**. "I'm off then, okay? Bye!"

---

remnant – Überrest; to lure away – weglocken; malicious – gehässig

I ran out of the kitchen and grabbed the bag with my bikini and towel. That **blasted** Holly! And Carlos! And those damned Grandfather stories! Did Holly really believe she could get me out of the way so easily? Full of anger, I pedalled like mad on my vintage bike.

I swept around the **bend**, and narrowly missed colliding with another cyclist. "Constantin! Hey, watch out!"

"You cut the corner," he said. "I was just coming to see you."

"Oh?"

"Yes."

I screwed up my eyes. "What have you got planned? I'm going to the beach. You can come if you like."

"Nothing I'd rather do!" He grinned happily. "It's exactly what I wanted."

"What? A morning on the beach?"

"No. I wanted you to say that I could come with you."

"Off we go! What are you waiting for?"

By the time we were parking our bikes, my red-hot anger had turned cold. I knew one thing for certain: I had no desire to **assert** myself constantly against other girls who fell for Carlos. Of course, there would always be Wandas and Hollys, just as there would always be Jonnys and Constantins. But I wasn't going to enter into this game. I had made a decision. It was over with Carlos. I would have a

---

blasted – verdammt; bend – Kurve;
to assert – sich behaupten, sich durchsetzen

couple of nice days here collecting material, and I wouldn't lose sight of my goal – to become the most famous travel writer of all time – for a single second longer. *One* Wanda experience was enough for me. A second was completely unnecessary.

As we were tramping through the dunes, Constantin cautiously reached for my hand. "I was thinking about you all night," he said quietly.

"What? Couldn't you sleep? You must be completely exhausted, Constantin."

He shook his head. "Quite the opposite. Hey, what's Carlos up to?"

"He's investigating the Morsum Cliff. With Holly," I replied.

Constantin didn't reply.

There were **heaps of** people on the beach already. The wind was still, and it was sunny and warm. The weather changes here more quickly than it does at home in the south.

"Do you fancy a swim?" asked Constantin.

The question was completely justified. "I don't imagine it can get any nicer than this," I said. "I'll just get changed quickly, okay? I'll be back in a moment. That is, Constantin ..." I hesitated. "Have you actually got your **swimming trunks** with you?"

"I've got them on ... under my jeans," he replied, embarrassed. I grinned with relief. The boy was just as against the idea of **skinny-dipping** as I was.

We paddled and splashed and swam and let the waves carry us out and back onto the sand again. It

---

heaps of – haufenweise; swimming trunk – Badehose; skinny-dipping – Nacktbaden

was simply fabulous, and when we were finally sitting on the sand again, I'd forgotten that I was angry with Carlos and Holly ... well, no, I hadn't actually forgotten it.

But I did manage not to think about it the whole time. Constantin and I baked in the sun and talked about everything that seemed important to us. I discovered that he lived in Wiesbaden and didn't have any brothers or sisters. His father had wanted him to study Law, but he didn't fancy it. "I know for a fact that I don't want to do that under any circumstances. But I don't know for sure what I *do* want to do. Maybe ... I'd most like ..." He laughed, embarrassed, and said, "At any rate, I do know that I'm hungry and thirsty now."

"Me, too," I said. "And I'll get a sunburn if I lie here any longer."

"Let's see ... Yes, your arms are already red, you know. Your neck, too. But your nose has got it worst."

He bent down over me and kissed me. His kiss was very tender. Lovely.

He also stroked my sunburnt arms and I have to say I didn't mind in the slightest. Quite the opposite.

Constantin had some money. We had spaghetti with chilli and then – the hotness of the chillis must have got my mind working overtime – I invited Constantin to come with me to see Holly's grandfather. The information was very important to me, and the sooner I could begin my life without Carlos, the better. In any case, the three to five hours that Holly had **estimated** for the visit to the

---

to estimate – schätzen

damned Morsum Cliff weren't up yet, and if Carlos were to see me with Constantin – against all the probabilities of time – then that was exactly what I intended.

Holly's grandfather was sitting in a quiet corner away from the wind, having a doze. But Elli, Holly's mother, awoke him without any **pangs of conscience**.

"You've got visitors, Mimi and ... Are you Carlos? You looked different the last time I saw you."

I introduced him. "This is Constantin." I'd actually wanted to say, "my boyfriend". But I bit it back and reminded myself energetically that I was going to change my life completely and radically. When I was in Chile, I carried a red card around with me. "My heart is done for! I'll never fall in love again!" it said. I had **strayed from** my resolution once, but what do you learn from your mistakes? Precisely.

"I want to be the most famous travel writer of all time," I explained coolly. "At home, I work for the teen pages of our newspaper, and I've been **commissioned** to write several articles about life on the island. Albrecht said you'd be able to sort me out with some stories." Not bad, I praised myself silently. Mimi, you did that well!

"So, that's what Albrecht says?" Tom Thoms was even older, even more wrinkled, and even smaller than Albrecht. He took his cold pipe out of his mouth, looked at it **in disgust**, and put it next to him on the bench. "Why didn't Holly come with you?"

---

pang of conscience – Gewissensbiss; to stray from sth – von etwas abkommen; to commission – beauftragen; in disgust – angeekelt

"She said she knows all the stories," I replied, hoping that it was true. "And in any case, she's showing Carlos the Morsum Cliff."

"No!" her grandfather cried. "That little ... So *that's* why my guide-book to the island is missing! Look at that, so that's how it is!" He gave me a piercing look, but I didn't avoid his **gaze**.

"Of course. She said she knows her stuff. Her geological stuff, that is. Carlos is studying Geology, so he's more interested in faults than he is in stories."

Tom Thoms stuck his cold pipe back in his mouth. "That means ..." He really did have a penetrating look, but I'd rather have exploded than let him see that I was cursing Holly to hell and back. "That means the stories aren't empty excuses?"

"No! I need them!" I cried.

He shuffled back inside the house, returning with a big black book. "I've written down all the stories I've collected over my lifetime in here."

Oh God! My heart sank down into my boots. This would be fun!

Constantin came to my rescue. "We don't want to take up too much of your time. We're particularly interested in **seafaring** stories."

"We?" repeated Tom Thoms.

"Yes. I might become," Constantin turned a bit red, "a writer. But I've never told anyone that before."

"What?" I almost fell off my chair. "Constantin! Is that why you read so much?"

He nodded.

"Didn't you know?" asked Tom Thoms.

---

gaze – Blick; seafaring – Seefahrer-

I shook my head and placed my notebook on the table, at the ready. "Constantin and I have only known one another for a couple of days."

"Ah, well ... let me have a quick think ... So you want to hear seafaring stories. Well, there are loads of them. There's the one about the sailor who spent his entire life cruising around the oceans of the world for more than 50 years. And when he finally became too old, he took a train to Flensburg to sort out the paperwork. But barely had his feet touched the land when he was killed by a tram. Poor chap, that one. He wasn't afraid of the devil or the water. The tram was his doom."

Tom Thoms drew on his cold pipe and I hurried to note down the most important words.

"Then there's a famous story. Two men from Sylt meet in Africa –"

"What?" I asked in amazement, putting my pen down.

Tom Thoms grinned. "Just a moment. I need to tell you what happened beforehand. When they were just ten or twelve, the boys signed up for merchant ships which collected **spices**, palm-oil, **china**, **silk** and other **valuable** goods on the shores of Africa and East Asia. The fully loaded ships were, of course, a much **sought-after haul** for pirates. They boarded the ships, the crew were taken prisoner and either bought off by the shipping companies or, if **the latter** had **gone bankrupt** or weren't interested in their people, offered

---

spices – Gewürze; china – Porzellan; silk – Seide;
valuable – wertvoll; sought-after – gefragt; haul – Beute;
the latter – Letzterer; to go bankrupt – bankrott gehen

on the slave market. One ship with a Sylt boy named Tam Tamen on it was captured in 1746 by African pirates. Tamen ended up in slavery, but because he was a bright boy, he made it to become leader of a group of wild Saharan **warriors** and one day discovered an imprisoned ship's boy on the slave market in Algeria. 'Aren't you a Sylt boy?' he's supposed to have said in Frisian, before buying him his liberty."

"Just imagine that, Constantin! If it had been you!"

"Who? The little slave or the desert prince?"

"**Take your pick**. So are there any stories about women or girls?"

Tom Thoms finally filled his pipe. "There's the wrecker story of Ellen Mannis." He drew and drew, but his pipe had its own mind. "You need to know," he stated when it was finally alight, "since 1705 the punishment for wrecking had been the death penalty. But, as I said, the Sylt people were poor. They could make use of anything that the sea threw up onto the beach. For them, **flotsam and jetsam** was a **blessing** and compensation for what the sea took from them. 'God bless our beach', the Sylt people are said to have prayed, and sometimes the sea gave to them **in abundance**; in just one night in October 1881, four ships ran aground."

Tom Thoms held his lighter to his pipe again. "Merchant ships, you must realise, were little sailing ships which were entirely dependent on the

---

warrior – Krieger; Take your pick. – Such's dir aus.;
flotsam and jetsam – Treibgut; blessing – Segen;
in abundance – in Hülle und Fülle

weather, since people could only calculate **degrees of latitude** at that time. The timber of the smashed-up ships was made into houses and stables; the planks were made into flooring, and the beams into posts.

Special **adjudicators** were posted on the beach to ensure that the **booty** was shared out fairly. This was a difficult job; they **fell between all the stools**, and couldn't do right by anyone. The job was dangerous, too; at one point, the people from Rantum were so angry with their Strandvogt that they stabbed him to death at his own wedding.

But you wanted to hear a story about a woman, Mimi. Ellen Mannis was a young widow who spotted a washed-up **butter-churn**. Unfortunately, the adjudicator saw her rolling her haul across the sand to safety. He shouted to her, to ask her what she had got, and only one way of keeping the man at a distance occurred to her in her moment of need: clothes off! Naked as she was, she kept the adjudicator at arm's length. Then," he drew on his pipe, "that was evidently off-putting. Ah, how **customs** change with the times!"

"And? How did the story end? Did Ellen get to keep the butter-churn? Did the adjudicator push off?"

"History doesn't tell us that."

Tom Thoms fell silent. He lost himself in thought, and finally knocked his pipe out. I looked

---

degree of latitude – Breitengrad; adjudicator – Schiedsrichter; booty – Beute; to fall between all the stools – zwischen allen Stühlen sitzen; butter-churn – Butterfass; custom – Sitte, Brauch

surreptitiously at the clock and realized that Holly and Carlos had been gone for seven hours. That pretty much said it all ...

"The things people do to one another," Tom Thoms said now, as if he had read my thoughts. "In 1713, a stranded fisherman from Archsum rescued himself and his money-box with great difficulty by the shore. Wreckers discovered him, **beat him up**, and **buried** him in the sand. However, he was only half-dead, and stretched his arm accusingly out of the sand. So the robbers chopped his arm off and fled with the **loot**. Since then, the fisherman has been wandering around the island as a ghost with a bloody stump for an arm."

Groaning, Tom Thoms stood up. "So, that's all for today. All this talking makes me tired. Come round again another day."

"Thank you!"

"Ah, you **landlubbers** may not know this," was his parting shot. "But the business about the flotsam and jetsam was so organized that the **authorities** were **entitled to** two-thirds of the **salvaged** goods, later only one third."

"And who were the authorities?" asked Constantin.

Tom Thoms didn't reply. He shuffled back into his house.

---

to beat sb up – jmdn. zusammenschlagen; to bury – begraben; loot – Beute; landlubber – Landratte; authorities – Behörden; to be entitled to – Anspruch haben auf; to salvage – bergen

Dangerous pirates!

"What now?" asked Constantin. "Do you want to go home?"

That was the very last thing I wanted to do. "Why would I want to do that?"

We pushed our bikes along the street. "Have you ever been to List? The northernmost point of the island?"

"Not yet. What are you waiting for? The night is still young!" We had a **tail wind**. Imagine that!

At List harbour, there was a kiosk selling shrimps. Constantin bought a bagful and showed me how to get the flesh out of the shells. "**Peeling**," it's called. It's a nice but rather funny way to spend your time; the more you eat, the hungrier you become. But I only realized that later on. We sat on a little bench with a view over the water, peeled, and watched a cutter chugging into the harbour. On board were chic little pirates in little red and white striped shirts and red head-scarves, complete with **skull** and cross-bones. They were all waving metal **sabres** and yelling "Ahoy" and "Mum" and "Dad".

---

tail wind – Rückenwind; peeling – *hier:* pulen;
skull – Totenkopf; sabre – Säbel

"I thought carnival was in February," I said, astonished.

As the cutter **berthed**, hordes of parents welcomed their little ones. "That was brilliant," **gushed** an ex-pirate. "We fought for a treasure-map! And we had to **haul** a **chest** on board, full of sweeties!"

"Yes, but the best thing is the Pirate's Patent!" His brother was waving an impressive-looking **parchment**.

"Did you get it just like that?" asked the Mum.

"Course not, we had to do loads of things for it. Peel shrimps and tie people up and **swear like a trooper**. Swearing was the best."

"I bet you got the first prize," conjectured the proud father.

"Not likely! Laura **nabbed** that one. She was best at tying people up, and she knew most swear-words. It's always the girls ..."

"That's life," said Constantin next to me. "That kid knows what's what. Do you know that joke, Mimi? A man's sitting on a bench and a **fairy** comes along and says, 'You may make a wish.' – 'I want to be more **cunning**,' says the man. 'No problem,' replies the fairy – and **hey presto**! a woman is sitting on the bench."

"Ha!" I flashed my eyes at Constantin. "So how come you're still a boy? You presumably **failed** to say hello when you encountered the fairy?"

---

to berth – anlegen; to gush – schwärmen; to haul – ziehen; chest – Kiste; parchment – Pergament; to swear like a trooper – höllisch fluchen; to nab – schnappen, erwischen; fairy – Fee; cunning – schlau; hey presto – plötzlich; to fail – versagen

"Failed to? When I saw her floating through the air, I **deliberately** said nothing. I knew, you see, that I would at some point meet exactly the kind of super-girl that you are," retorted Constantin. He moved close to me and put his arm round my shoulders.

"Constantin, you're really **quick-witted**!"

"Not just quick-witted. At the right moment I can keep my mouth shut, too." He leant over to me, but I turned my face away. Not because I wanted to **mess him around**, but firstly, because I still had a mouthful of shrimp, and secondly, because I didn't particularly want to be **smooching** amidst sabre-**brandishing** mini pirates. And then the business with Carlos was still lying heavily on my shoulders.

As it was starting to get dark, we got back on our bikes, but I caught a look at a poster: "Endless Summer Party Night."

I braked sharply and read: Kampen, 9pm.

"Constantin! Do you have to get back to your mother?"

"I've got to **put in an appearance** at breakfast tomorrow morning. Why?"

"Do you fancy going to a party?"

"With you, any time!"

In my **current** state of mind, this answer did me as much good as a trip to a trendy health **spa**.

---

deliberate – freiwillig; quick-witted – schlagfertig; to mess sb around – jmdn. an der Nase herumführen; to smooch – knutschen, schmusen; to brandish – schwingen; to put in an appearance – in Erscheinung treten; current – momentan; spa – Kurbad

We pedalled like mad and could soon hear from a distance the music near 'Buhne 16'. Boy, that was some party; it was a non-stop party! The music was banging, techno noise was **booming**, reggae was in there somewhere, and so was Afro-jazz. The beach was **heaving**; the lights were flashing; and the waves were clapping along. The guy in front of me had pulled out of his wardrobe the hugest baggy trousers you've ever seen, and when he moved even just slightly, I got a full view of the **waistband** of some 'in' underpants. Fab. His companion –

"Oh God! Does it have to be? Johanna ..."

I quickly pulled Constantin away. "I can't be doing with her tonight."

It was the best party night of my life. Constantin was lost in **admiration**; he didn't take his eyes off me for a second. He was sweet. **Attentive**. And he'd have been the perfect boyfriend if he hadn't kept looking at me so lovingly.

Long after midnight we found a quiet little spot in the dunes. Admittedly, we weren't alone: there were other people whispering, giggling and laughing everywhere, and they all needed the same as us: a little break.

The music did still reach our ears, but we could hear the surf and the wind, too. Constantin bent over me and whispered all the things into my ear that people say when they've just fallen in love.

I didn't say anything. **At the most**, I occasionally said "Hmmm" or brushed his hair off his fore-

---

to boom – dröhnen; to heave – wogen; waistband – Hosenbund, Bündchen; admiration – Bewunderung; attentive – aufmerksam; at the most – höchstens

head as it kept falling over his eyes. At some point he noticed.

"Don't you feel the same?" he asked quietly. "Are you as happy as I am?"

"I wasn't listening," I whispered. "Can you hear the surf?"

"I wish I had thousands of shooting stars to give to you," he replied, kissing me non-stop. "I'd give you the moon from the sky and the most beautiful pearls from the deepest depths of the ocean if it were possible. So that I can see your face and your eyes, the sea should shine and –"

"Talk to the noctiluca miliaris," a voice resounded from the darkness. "The creature is capable of **bioluminescence** – a chemical **combustion** process that produces a faint light. Okay?"

If I'd been in love with Constantin, the **unsolicited** interruption would have bothered me enormously. As it was, I giggled at first, then laughed so much that Constantin held his hand over my mouth and said, "Shh!"

"What a pain," he grumbled. "During my first declaration of love, of all moments, someone has to **butt in** with his glowing **protozoa**!"

"He meant well! He just wanted to help you; after all, you did say you wanted a bit of light!"

Later on I crept barefoot into my room. No idea whether Carlos was in his bed. And it didn't have anything to do with me any more, did it?

---

bioluminescence – Biolumineszenz; combustion – Verbrennung; unsolicited – ungewollt, unaufgefordert; to butt in – sich einmischen; protozoan – Urtierchen

Naffed off

= - = - = - = - =

When I appeared in the kitchen next morning, Märthe ran her hand over my head **with concern** and lapsed into her native dialect. "Seems to me you're a bit naffed off. You drink your coffee, then you'll feel better."

"Where are the others?"

"Albrecht is on the beach with Noballs."

"And ... Carlos?" I asked as casually as possible.

"He's still asleep." Märthe placed three fried eggs in front of my nose.

"Thanks, but not for me."

She said something in her own dialect.

"So what does that mean? I don't understand a word!"

"My God, how am I supposed to translate that!" Märthe frowned.

"Does it mean something like: food and drink keep body and soul together?"

"Maybe, maybe not." She scrutinized me so **uninhibitedly** that I felt really stupid and uncomfortable. "What's the matter?"

---

naffed off – weggetreten; with concern – besorgt; uninhibited – hemmungslos

"Well, my great-grandfather was a seaman," she explained, holding the plate of fried eggs under my nose. "He sailed to Asia and was also in China at one point. He brought back a **saying** from there. He did have china and silk in his luggage as well, but the saying was his favourite of all the things he brought back."

"Oh? It must have been particularly wise."

"Indeed. It was about **dragons** rising up."

"So what was it?" I raised my head. I could hear the floorboards creaking above me, couldn't I? Yes, and the **loo** flushing! Carlos was up. He was the last person I wanted to see now. I jumped up. "Bye, Märthe! I won't be able to force a single thing down today, honestly!"

At the door, she caught me after all. "The dragon only rises up against the wind!"

"Sorry?"

"The saying, Mimi! I just quickly wanted to tell you what it was."

I banged the door behind me and raced off. Only when I got to the third street corner did I realize that I'd forgotten my bike and had gone the wrong way. This way led to the **tidal flats**, didn't it? Never mind, I said to myself. After all, I need to see those, too. I had soon left the last houses behind me. Or so I thought, but then I saw another one **nestling** in a **hollow**. It looked sweet.

The nature reserve began then, and I hesitated. Should I go left or right? I discovered a path leading

---

saying – Sprichwort; dragon – Drache; loo – Klo;
tidal flats – Wattenmeer; to nestle – sich schmiegen;
hollow – Vertiefung

through the heather, jumped down it, kept to the left and was standing on the path to the tidal flats.

The wind was completely still, and it was very warm. **Dense** white clouds covered the sky, and it looked as if it might rain soon. Sweat stood out on my forehead. The path was such that I never got to the water. I eventually found myself standing on a second bridge that led through wet fields with dense grassy bushes that I didn't recognize. Water was everywhere, and the whole thing looked pretty **unappealing** and **swampy**.

I sat at the end of the bridge, dangling my legs.

Märthe and her great-grandfather's saying, "The dragon only rises up against the wind." What did that mean? Did it mean: resistance makes you strong? Or: only resistance brings you further? It presumably had to be something along those lines.

I looked around. There was nobody to be seen; they were probably all still sleeping after the long summer night party. Hesitantly, I tapped the **slate**-grey sand. It was warm and hard. Completely hard. I stood **on tiptoe**. Far ahead of me the water was glistening, but the ground was practically dry and covered in little spaghetti-like heaps. The tip of a **tail** suddenly shot out of a circular hole – and at that moment a gull shot down, made a **lunge**, and flew off at top speed with its **prey**, a wriggling worm.

Cautiously, I groped my way along. A little crab scurried to safety in front of me with its peculiar

---

dense – dicht; unappealing – nicht ansprechend; swampy – morastig, sumpfig; slate – Schiefer; on tiptoe – auf Zehenspitzen; tail – Schwanz; lunge – Stoß; prey – Beute

crooked gait. A little further along, some birds were **scrapping** about something I didn't recognize. There was a mussel here, a piece of seaweed there. I jumped over a **ditch** and something startled me. Peculiar: the sand was pretty soft here.

A few steps later, though, it was like a board, so I went on and on, always heading for the glistening surface of the water. Sometimes the sand was hard and uneven; sometimes as soft as mud.

After a while I turned round. Everything was okay: there was the beach, and I could also see the roofs of the houses.

Everything was all right, then ... But the stupid thing was that it was beginning to spit with rain. I had, of course, forgotten my anorak in my **haste** to get out of the house, but it wasn't possible to be any wetter than wet, I told myself as I looked at my watch. How on earth was I supposed to spend the day, I asked myself. Constantly **fleeing from** Carlos didn't make sense. I could call Constantin; I had his mobile number. But a further day alone with him brought new complications. I wondered and pondered, cursing Holly and that stupid Carlos, and then remembered my life goal. "I'm going to be the most famous travel writer ever," I growled finally. "I'm turning round and cycling to the editorial office of the Sylt paper. They can give me all the information they have on the modelling competition, then I'll go to the airport, **suss out** the location, and then we'll see what happens next."

---

crooked gait – schiefer Gang; to scrap – sich streiten; ditch – Graben; haste – Eile; to flee from sb – jmdm. entfliehen; to suss out – auskundschaften

Meanwhile the drizzle had turned into proper rain. I turned – and was standing next to a **stream**. Where did that come from? I could have sworn that it wasn't there a few minutes ago. And where were the roofs? They couldn't have **disappeared into thin air**, could they? They hadn't been a **mirage**. I may not know much about the island, but I was quite sure that it didn't **boast** mirages.

The rain poured down, the view was **atrocious**, and the sand beneath my feet was pretty soft.

I jumped over a **rivulet**, then over a second and a third. A fourth, wider one – almost a stream – forced me to take a **diversion**.

Suddenly, I couldn't see anything at all. It was as if a cloud had enveloped me. I tramped on. With every step, I could feel the sand becoming softer and softer. And wetter? Wetter, too. I took a **trial** step. My footprint immediately filled up with water. That hadn't been the case before. I started to feel frightened. My heart was beating so hard that it was actually drumming inside me. I stopped where I was, cursing. Over on the beach there were lifeguards who make sure people get out of the water when there's danger. And here, where it would be sensible to have lifeguards, they **chicken out**?! Does that make sense? No, it doesn't make sense!

Suddenly, against my will, I had to laugh. Mimi,

---

stream – Bach; to disappear into thin air – sich in Luft auflösen; mirage – Luftspiegelung; to boast sth – sich etwas rühmen; atrocious – scheußlich; rivulet – Flüsschen; diversion – Umweg; trial – Versuch, Probe; to chicken out – kneifen

I said to myself, this will make a great story. "Missing in the Mud! Rescued after three long days!"

Hey! What was that again? Didn't the water drag people out so far that even a good swimmer couldn't find his way back again? That thought made me feel quite ill, and my heart-rate stepped up a further gear.

But I didn't feel truly lousy until the water started **sloshing** around my shoes. My God, this really was dangerous! There was no use calling; I knew that the fog – or the clouds – swallowed up every sound. And I knew something else: I had in the meantime lost all sense of which direction the beach was in. What **a pain in the bum**!

I stood, staring at the white clouds, feeling the water around my ankles, and the fear inside me. A gull flew squawking over me; I raised my eyes reluctantly – and I could see something blue shining through!

A few moments later the cloud had disappeared. I saw that I had in fact been going in completely the wrong direction, namely towards the water. I turned round, ran to the bridge as fast as I could and reached safety with a single bound.

---

to slosh – schwappen; a pain in the bum – ein Ärgernis

I just know about solutions!

As the first houses came into view, the rain stopped. I bent to pull up my sock that kept slipping down, and was almost knocked over from behind. **For heaven's sake**, that's all I needed!

I turned round angrily. "Noballs! Where did you come from?" The dog barked happily, put his front paws on my shoulders and licked my face.

"Noballs! Could you please leave Mimi in peace? Behave yourself!"

Albrecht put Noballs on the lead. "We've been for our morning walk," he explained, then stopped short. "Mimi! Just look at you! Is something wrong?"

I grinned, embarrassed. "Nah. What makes you ask?"

He examined me. "It seems to me that you're **a tad** naffed off."

"That's what Märthe said, too," I murmured and walked on.

After a few metres Albrecht stopped. "You're out early," he said.

"I was in the flats."

---

for heaven's sake – um Himmels willen;
a tad – ein bisschen

"On your own? You shouldn't do that."

I nodded. "I didn't go out far. The sand was hard … but then a cloud came. And the rain." I swallowed.

"What do you know about the flats?" asked Albrecht.

"Nothing," I admitted.

"Nothing? That's what I thought." We stopped outside the white painted garden gate. "Why didn't Carlos go with you?"

"Because … when I went, he was still asleep." I was cross because Albrecht was blocking my way. He shook his head, was about to say something, then thought better of it. He pushed the gate open and tramped on ahead.

It was deadly silent in the house. The kitchen door was open, as was the door to the front room, the 'Piisel'.

"Come on, Mimi," said Albrecht. "Here's something for you to read."

He pulled a fat **tome** from a shelf, **flicked through** it, and pressed the book into my hand. "The tidal flats," it said.

"If Märthe asks where I am," said Albrecht, "I'll be back at lunchtime. Come on, Noballs."

A moment later the front door clicked shut.

I sank into Albrecht's leather armchair by the window and firstly pulled off my wet shoes and socks, then looked around. The **oak** table gleamed; the bluey-white tiles on the walls gleamed, and the sun that was now falling through the **panes** of the

---

tome – Band; to flick through – durchblättern;
oak – Eiche; pane – Scheibe

little windows onto the **brass** lights made the latter gleam, too. Everything was gleaming and shining, but inside me, dark night **prevailed**.

I sighed and read out of desperation – and because, in any case, I had nothing better to do – the information about the flats. "The tidal flats are **criss-crossed** by little channels. They form the water courses for the incoming and outgoing tides and never dry out, even at low tide ... The paths over the tidal flats mostly follow the **watersheds**, and the guides choose ones that ensure that people can wade through the channels at their shallower points and can **skirt round** mussel beds and tricky places that seem quite safe but are in fact **voids** covered by a thin **layer** of sand. The 'paths' constantly change and are therefore not marked. Anything such as sudden changes in the weather, storms, or **gathering** sea-**mists** become mortally dangerous just as they are in the mountains. Without expert guides and a compass, one should never go into the tidal flats –" A floorboard creaked and I raised my head. "Carlos! You **made me jump**!"

"Oh? Where were you this morning? And yesterday? And when did you get back last night?"

I couldn't believe it!

"Pardon? You push off and then want to know where I was? You're **off your rocker**!" I snapped,

---

brass – Messing; to prevail – sich durchsetzen;
to criss-cross – kreuzweise durchziehen; watershed – Wasserscheide; to skirt round – herumgehen um;
void – Loch; layer – Schicht; to gather – (sich) sammeln;
mist – Nebel; to make sb jump – jmdn. erschrecken;
to be off your rocker – übergeschnappt sein

jumping up. The book fell to the floor; we bent simultaneously to pick it up, and banged our heads together. "Ouch!"

Carlos grabbed my arm. "Mimi, you knew where I was. I didn't know where you were – and who you were out with. With Constantin? What did you two do?"

"What's it got to do with you? Nothing!"

"Oh yes, it has! You're my girlfriend –"

"I *used to be*," I interrupted him hotly.

Carlos stared at me. "Used to be? You said, you used to be? How am I supposed to take that?"

"Just as it's meant. I'm fed up with your Wandas and Hollys – and just completely fed up!"

"And what about your Jonnys and Constantins?" cried Carlos.

"**Tit for tat**!" I yelled.

"Mimi! What can I do about it if Holly –"

"Exactly," I interrupted him. "What can you do about it if Holly's in love with you and Constantin's in love with me?"

Carlos stopped short. "Are these natural events? Sudden changes that we're delivered up to like the weather? Pah!" He leant against the wall. "I thought we'd sorted all that out."

"Sorted what out? That you'll **ditch** me for any bird who looks adoringly at you?"

"That's not what I meant," stammered Carlos helplessly.

"No? So how was it meant? Something like, Mimi, dear, I'll bother about Holly for *now*, but I'll

---

Tit for tat. – Wie du mir, so ich dir.;
to ditch sb – wegwerfen

be there for you later on. Is that what you meant? Great, then I can keep up, Carlos."

He was silent, then he said quietly, "I don't get it. Other people manage it."

"What?"

"Being together without constantly quarrelling about other people."

"Of course," I retorted. "Of course, they manage it. They presumably do something different from us."

"But what?"

"Listen, Carlos, we don't just live together on a **remote** island. There will always be people who attach themselves to you or me and who want to disrupt things. So? We can't kill them. We can't run away from them either."

"So how do other people do it? We can't be the only ones like this, can we?" Carlos said so miserably that my heart felt all warm inside, and my anger with him disappeared in no time at all, like the cloud of mist had done not long ago.

"No." I bit my bottom lip. "We could, of course, say, Hey, everyone, we're together. Hands off us. Or we could hang a sign around our necks saying, 'I'm toxic! Keep your distance!'"

"That would really get me going, Mimi."

"Me, too, if I didn't have a boyfriend and fancied having one."

We came up with the maddest ideas, and finally got on to external signs: matching earrings or matching rings on our fingers, something along those lines.

---

remote – entlegen, einsam

"I don't want that," I protested. "Either I know that I belong to you, or –"

"It's not about you or me, Mimi. It's about other people," explained Carlos.

In Chile, I'd travelled around with the red card. It said on it: "I'll never fall in love again!" I'd made a yellow card for Sylt: "Real adventures happen in the mind." How true that was! I had thought that Carlos had had a great day with Holly yesterday – and he'd thought the same about Constantin and me. You'd need, I **mused**, something along these lines. You'd simply hold up a card that said: "Don't bother! I've got a boyfriend!" Then everyone would know what was what. Everyone could read.

"The fault lies with us, Carlos," I said. "We have to change. Look, there are all kinds of fantastic people who would ... you know. But you know who's **available** and who isn't, don't you?"

"Mmmm."

"So the question is: how do these fantastic people act?"

For the first time that morning, Carlos laughed. "Well, how do you think? The way I acted yesterday!"

"What did you do?"

"Simple. I told Holly that we were rock solid," explained Carlos.

I was flabbergasted. "So why are we fighting?" I **stammered**.

"Because you and Constantin –"

"It's not true!" I cried.

---

to muse – nachdenken; available – verfügbar;
to stammer – stammeln

"Did you tell him firmly that we belong together?" Carlos probed.

"Nnnnnot directly. I thought that you and Holly –"

"Crikey, Mimi, all she did was take me to the cliff!"

"Yes, that's what you think," I defended myself because I suddenly had a terribly **bad conscience**. "But her grandfather saw through her. The **wretched** creature read up in his tourist guide so she could impress you."

Carlos grinned. "And what trick did Constantin come up with to impress you?"

"He's just sweet," I said.

"Sweet? **Yuck**!"

"Have you two made up?" Märthe had slipped in unnoticed. She put down the fully laden shopping basket and placed a newspaper on the table.

"It was all just a misunderstanding," said Carlos.

"Misunderstandings are Schietkram." She sat herself in Albrecht's chair. "When my husband was still alive, there was always trouble at first about these misunderstandings. There was, you see, an old boyfriend who didn't want to admit that I'd married Hinrich. And then when Hinrich saw Carl even at a distance, you could see the anger rise on his face."

"How did you get over the trouble?" Carlos and I asked simultaneously.

"It took a while." Märthe looked out of the window. "It will get better," she said calmly. "Everyone

---

bad conscience – schlechtes Gewissen;
wretched – erbärmlich; Yuck! – Ekelhaft!

has to go through it. Either they believe one another, and it'll last, or they don't believe what the other says, and they don't last. It's that simple."

"The dragon only rises up against the wind," I said, **quoting** the Chinese saying that her great-grandfather had brought back from his travels.

"Absolutely. No love without resistance, and without resistance, no love," Märthe summed up the matter.

All the same, I grumbled, "I don't **give a toss about** resistance and disturbing influences."

"You cannot give a toss about all you like, but you can't **toss** it all **away**."

"What else can I do?"

Märthe shook her head to and fro. "What do I know? Everyone has to solve that problem for themselves."

The newspaper rustled. Carlos burst out laughing, pointed to a big headline, and read aloud, "It says: 'I don't know about problems, I just know about solutions.'"

"That's what I said! Stop moaning. Think instead about how you can deal with the resistance." Märthe stood up with a groan and rubbed her back. "So, I've got to make lunch now. What are you going to do?"

Before we could answer, the doorbell rang like mad.

---

to quote – zitieren; not to give a toss about sth – auf etwas pfeifen; to toss away – wegwerfen

It never rains but it pours

"Hi!" Holly was waving a bag. "Great swimming weather. Are you coming?"

"We're eating in an hour!" Märthe called from the kitchen. "Holly, there's enough for you, too, but be on time, okay? And just you lot watch out for Schietkram, do you hear?"

"What does she mean by Schietkram?" Holly asked immediately.

"That's Mimi's and my business," replied Carlos, running upstairs to fetch his swimming things.

"Okay." Holly put her head on one side. "Are you cross with me, Mimi?"

"Obviously I was cross with you yesterday. You shouldn't have made off with Carlos like that, should you? But I got my revenge."

Holly nodded. "Carlos suspected as much yesterday. He was very angry with you, I can tell you! And with me. He said I should kindly stick to the rules. But ...," she grinned, "... but it's mostly the case that boys don't miss out on anything, don't you reckon? At least that's always been my experience."

---

to pour – schütten

Holly was so **straight-up** that you couldn't be angry with her.

I shrugged my shoulders and went red; after all, I hadn't exactly behaved in an exemplary manner yesterday. "So? Are you going to stick to the rules now?"

"Of course. What choice do I have?"

"Glad you see it like that," I remarked. "I've got my eye on you – got it?"

We rode down Alte Dorfstraße and waited for the little green man at the traffic lights. When he appeared, we leapt back onto our bikes and pedalled off. Behind us we could hear the jangling of a **rusty** bicycle bell. Someone wanted to pass us, but it didn't occur to us to clear out of the way.

"Hey, are you **deaf**?"

Oh God, it was Constantin. He was all I needed. "You go on ahead, okay?" I asked the others quickly. "We'll catch you up."

Carlos threw me a look that clearly said, "Watch out for Schietkram, Mimi!" Oh, just get stuck in, I decided. But I felt uncomfortable all the same.

"Hey, Constantin!"

"Mimi!" Constantin rode so close to me that he could put his arm around me.

"I've brought you something. This is for you." He handed me a rather **dishevelled** red **dog rose**.

"Thanks." This whole business was becoming increasingly **dodgy**! I **screwed up** all my courage.

---

straight-up – geradeheraus; rusty – rostig; deaf – taub; dishevelled – zerzaust; dog rose – Heckenrose; dodgy – vertrackt; to screw up – *hier:* zusammennehmen

"Constantin, yesterday evening was a mistake. Forget everything you whispered to me in the dunes, okay?"

"But why? I've fallen in love with you, and I thought –"

"You thought wrongly," I interrupted him. "It's my fault, I know. I'm sorry, truly sorry, but you know, Carlos and I ..."

I stopped, then had another go. "Carlos is the only one for me, you know?"

"No, I don't know," replied Constantin, confused. "But yesterday evening you said –"

"Constantin, I made a mistake." I **dismounted**. "I was so angry with Carlos that I really did want to finish with him, but I was wrong; the whole thing was just a misunderstanding. It was a mistake," I insisted.

"It was a mistake," repeated Constantin tonelessly. It was terrible to have to watch his disappointment growing and growing. I made a resolution that was to last for ever and all time: that I would never fool around with anyone else, regardless of how angry I was with Carlos. "Come on, **be a sport**," I asked. "Be my friend, will you?"

He looked at the ground, then at me; stretched his arm out, and I did think he really wasn't angry with me. But then, all of a sudden, he turned and pedalled off, and I was left standing there gawping stupidly after him.

"Constantin!" I overtook him and blocked his way. "Crikey, Constantin, don't be angry. We've only known one another for three days!"

---

to dismount – absteigen; Be a sport. – Sei nicht so.

"So? Time doesn't play any role."

"Yes, it does. Time does play a role. Look, I've already experienced so much with Carlos. We met in Chile; we survived an **earthquake**; we've been to Marrakech and in the Abruzzi – that sort of thing **welds** you **together**. Can't you see that?"

"Yesterday evening – why were you so ... I mean, you acted as if I meant something to you."

"Yes, that's all true. I told you, though, that it was a mistake!"

Constantin shook his head and got back on his bike. "I have to **digest** all this first."

Helplessly, I watched him as he pedalled off through the sand.

Carlos and Holly were waiting at the foot-bridge which led down to the beach.

"Where's Constantin?" Holly asked immediately.

"He didn't want to come."

"Why not?" **needled** Holly.

I shook my head stubbornly and didn't reply.

"Have you treated him **shabbily**?" Holly asked directly. "Because you thought something was going on between Carlos and me?"

I felt damned uncomfortable. "Something like that ..." I murmured.

"Really? Blimey, Mimi, first of all Johanna, whom he can't stand, clings to him like chewing gum. He thinks Johanna is foul, and falls in love with you. But you're in love with Carlos, and you give Constantin the push as soon as you know that

---

earthquake – Erdbeben; to weld together – zusammenschweißen; to digest – verdauen; to needle – sticheln; shabby – schäbig

Carlos is sticking with you. That's tough." Holly stopped short. "Just a moment!" She threw her bag of swimming things down at my feet and ran back along the path.

"Has she **gone** completely **round the bend**?" Carlos asked.

"I don't think so. It's just one of her snap decisions. That is, it's **bound to** be about one of her favourite **pastimes**: organizing other people's lives."

"That might take some time," Carlos remarked.

I felt awful.

We took our clothes off and put our swimming things on. Neither Holly nor Constantin was anywhere to be seen.

We walked along the beach and collected mussels. The pair were nowhere around.

We threw ourselves into the waves, swam and splashed around, but it wasn't any fun – there was no Holly and no Constantin standing waving in the sand.

We dried ourselves off and got dressed.

We stuffed our wet swimming things in the plastic bags and stuck the bags into the **carriers** on our bikes: no Holly, no Constantin.

We cycled off, crossed the road, cruised down Alte Dorfstraße, turned into Sjipwai, and braked outside Albrecht's little white-painted gate. Two bikes were leaning against the wall.

---

to go round the bend – einen Knall haben;
to be bound to – etwas bestimmt tun;
pastime – Zeitvertreib; carrier – Gepäckträger

"It's that kind of a day," I murmured and slipped into the house.

Holly was helping Märthe in the kitchen. I could see through the window that Albrecht and Constantin were sitting in the garden. "Looks as if there's a man-to-man conversation going on. Albrecht's rummaging around in the great **wealth** of his life-experiences and is helping the poor deserted and **spurned** one to find his way back to life again," I whispered into Carlos' ear.

"Mimi, are you of all people **mocking them**?!" Carlos was frankly horrified. "That's mean."

"I'm not mean," I defended myself. "It's just my stupid attempt to come to terms with this Schietkram."

"The Schietkram is all your doing," Carlos reminded me.

"You're heartless! All I said was that people didn't have to stick together like two pieces of chewing gum. It's possible to spend a day with someone else every now and then, isn't it? But it wasn't part of the deal that Holly would fall in love with you!"

"Mimi, just stop going on about it! You thought Holly was Wanda Number Two, and you gave Constantin the come-on. That was mean and unfair."

"Are you two quarrelling again?" Märthe called from the kitchen. "Leave all that Schietkram and come and eat."

"Schietkram, Schietkram, Schietkram," I groaned. "Everything's Schietkram! I've lost my appetite."

---

wealth – Reichtum; to spurn – verschmähen;
to mock sb – sich lustig machen über jmdn.

Holly fetched Albrecht and Constantin; we sat at the table, and when Märthe brought in the baked fish, I suddenly realized that I was starving despite all the Schietkram.

"I cycled in the wrong direction at first," explained Holly. "But then I saw Constantin outside the *Village Pitcher*, and then Albrecht came along with Noballs and said we should come and wait for you here. What shall we do after we've eaten? I suggest I show you the *Silberkanne*. It's a former bunker which you absolutely have to see."

I screwed up my nose, but before I could say anything, Constantin said, "I'm not –"

"No question of you chickening out," Holly interrupted him. "Of course, you're coming with us. Or do you want to hang around your swimming pool and **mope**? Or keep Johanna company? You can't be that stupid, Constantin."

"You're organizing my life again," he complained.

"Of course. If I don't do it, you'll die of boredom."

"I've never been bored in my life! I read!"

Holly waved him aside. "Plenty of time for that! Letters don't have legs; they will stay nicely put on the page and wait for you to come back home."

Albrecht laughed. "Constantin, if I were you I'd not miss the *Silberkanne*."

He put a fish-bone on the edge of his plate. "Holly, I was at your grandfather's this morning. He's coming to tea on Sunday afternoon. You're invited, as of course are you, Constantin. I'd be very

---

to mope – Trübsal blasen

glad if your mother would like to accompany you. When are you leaving?"

"In a week," replied Constantin, brushing his hair away from his forehead. "What if my mother's already doing something?"

"Please do tell her that I've specially requested that she come."

"Do you know her?" asked Holly curiously.

"How should I know? I'd have to see her to know that," Albrecht replied **evasively**.

"True," Holly **conceded**.

We ate red fruit pudding and helped Märthe with the clearing up.

---

evasive – ausweichend; to concede – nachgeben

The Silberkanne

Whilst the others went to fetch their bikes, I quickly ran up to my room to fetch my rucksack, together with my notebook and camera. You never knew whether you might discover something **tremendously** exciting.

It isn't far from Sjipwai to the *Silberkanne*, but only a joker could give a former bunker such a posh name. We parked our bikes and listened to Holly's explanation. "So, there was a **barrow** here once upon a time. A barrow is a grave dating back to ancient history over which people shovelled a mountain of earth so that it was visible for miles around. Afterwards, nothing more happened here for a long time. Only during the last war was a bunker built on this spot, and after the war, when it wasn't needed any more, **refugees** fled to it. Fifty years ago somebody came up with the brilliant idea of turning the bunker into a guest-house. He planted all sorts of trees, bushes and **shrubs**, and arranged the garden in such a way that little niches and corners appeared everywhere. Come on, we might find a free table."

---

tremendous – gewaltig, riesig; barrow – Grabhügel; refugee – Flüchtling; shrub – Strauch

I threw my rucksack over my back and followed the others.

The former bunker was a lowly thatched building full of **nooks** and **crannies**, nestled right down in the dunes. To the right of it was a coffee garden. The tables, arranged either alone or in little groups, stood as if **enchanted** between the bushes and hedges. Two boys jumped up from their chairs and waved. "Dirk and Kai, the two lifeguards," cried Holly. "Why aren't you at the beach?"

"Today is our day off!" explained Dirk. "Come and sit with us. How come you're not in the water? What with this lovely weather!"

"We've already been swimming," I explained, putting my rucksack next to my chair. "And in any case, Holly wanted to show us the *Silberkanne*."

"The *Silberkanne* has one great advantage: you just see **greenery**, nothing of the guests, and above all no water," Kai said with a laugh. "Just a bit of the tidal flats, but I'd have to get up and go round the bush to see them." He demonstrated his point. "Like this, you see? ... Help! She's back! I think she's following us!" He sank down onto his chair and covered his eyes with his hands.

"Who do you mean?" I asked.

"It has to be that Johanna." Dirk peeped cautiously above the **branches**. "It is her. Calm down, Kai, she's got company."

Holly laughed. "What have you actually got against her?"

"She spends her whole day walking up and down

---

nook – Ecke; cranny – Winkel; enchanted – verzaubert; greenery – Grün; branch – Zweig

the beach, keeping a look-out for important people. She's particularly looking for people from the papers. She only comes to **annoy** us when there's nobody better **in the offing**. Oh well, she's leaving on Sunday. Then the big event will be over, too," said Kai.

"The modelling competition?"

"Precisely that." Kai finished his latte. "Are you taking part?"

"Are you stupid?" Holly and I **tapped our foreheads**.

"Why? Johanna's chances would be drastically reduced, and anyway, the whole thing is sure to be great fun."

Constantin, who had remained silent thus far, suddenly said, "Hey, that's a great idea. Mimi, you look fantastic, and Holly is an exotic beauty. You two would be guaranteed to steal the show from Johanna."

"That's what I say. But you could join in, too." Kai screwed up his eyes. "And you, too, Carlos. You'd be the perfect Latin Lover."

We all **roared**. Unfortunately. Everyone's heads turned to our table, and of course, Johanna had immediately spotted us.

She **steered** her way towards us and, as always, came straight to the point. "Mimi, there you are! The interview's still on, isn't it? It's Thursday today. It absolutely has to be in the papers tomorrow, as the show is on Saturday. So, when have you got time?"

---

to annoy – ärgern; in the offing – in Sicht;
to tap your forehead – sich an die Stirn tippen;
to roar – laut lachen; to steer – steuern

"When have *you* got time?" She had completely taken me by surprise.

"Now," she said coolly.

"Now? You can't just drop your companion!"

"I'm sure he'll be able to wait a few minutes," she said casually.

"Well, off you go, Mimi, get stuck in," Kai said **snidely**.

"Get it over with," said Carlos, grinning.

I couldn't fight the mob. I thought for a moment and decided that such an interview would be quite a good way into a report on the modelling competition. I immediately got my notebook out of my rucksack. "Okay, Johanna, let's find a quiet corner. Come on."

"I'll just quickly let that guy know."

When Johanna had gone, Holly asked, "Why don't you stay here? We'll help you to ask the right questions."

"No, no, I want to **savour** this fun on my own."

"What a shame!"

I laughed and got going. Johanna and I found a little place in the sun; I took out my pen, and before I could even open my mouth, Johanna was already rattling off her **measurements** and spitting out further information. "I speak three languages and my hobbies are golf and riding."

"What? You ride and even play golf? I've only ever seen you on the beach here."

"So? You can't do everything at the same time, can you?" she replied **pertly**.

---

snide – abfällig; to savour – auskosten;
measurement – Maß; pert – vorlaut, keck

"So how long have you been riding?" Now I wanted to know exactly how long.

"Since forever ..." she said evasively.

"Have you got your own horse?"

"Of course!"

"So what's his name?"

"Erm ... Silver Arrow."

"He must be a grey."

"A grey? Why should he be a grey?"

"Well, you certainly wouldn't call a black horse Silver Arrow. He'd more likely be Black Lightning or Blacky."

"Oh, I get it! Yes, of course, Silver Arrow is a grey."

I rolled my eyes. If I had my own horse, I'd know what he was called if my name wasn't Mimi Muschalek! Everything Johanna served up to me was to be **taken with a** large **pinch of salt**. I decided to quiz her a bit further. "Where is Silver Arrow?"

"Well, in the stable!"

"I assumed that much." I grinned encouragingly. "Sorry, I should have put it more precisely. It's undoubtedly interesting for the reader to know if your family has its own stables. I mean, that would be a real killer. Who can afford their own stables?"

Johanna looked me in the eye, laughing. "Having my own stables is so self-evident that I never even give it a moment's thought any more."

"Wow! Then you must have more than one horse, mustn't you?"

"Nnno, unfortunately not." Johanna pulled a face. "You know, after my mother had her riding accident, my father sold all the remaining horses."

---

to take sth with a pinch of salt – mit Vorsicht genießen

Oh fantastic, Johanna had read too many bad horse books – guaranteed!

"How terrible. That must have been an awful accident."

"Oh yes. I don't want to talk about it."

I acted **sympathetic**, sorry that I couldn't get a tear to run down my cheek. That would have given the **slushy** story a real bit of **zip**. I sighed deeply and changed the subject.

"You've presumably been playing golf since you were ten!"

"To be honest, I only started here."

"You booked a lesson?"

Johanna opened her eyes wide. "How do you know that?"

I was fed up with Johanna's **cock-and-bull stories**. My patience **vanished** and I snapped – which, of course, was completely unprofessional, "Blimey, Johanna, then you don't play golf – you're just learning to play it!"

"You don't have to let everyone in on everything," she replied coolly. "And in any case, there's no harm in me stretching the truth a bit, is there?"

I swallowed. "The stupid thing is that show-offs mostly get found out. But that's your problem." What could I ask next? I couldn't think of anything, but Johanna didn't need any help. "I'm sure readers will be interested to know what I do for my appearance." Crikey, I'd never have thought of that one! "Well, I go jogging every day; I eat fruit and

---

sympathetic – mitfühlend; slushy – sentimental;
zip – Pep; cock-and-bull story – Lügengeschichte;
to vanish – verschwinden

vegetables **by the bucketload**; I don't smoke; I don't drink alcohol –"

"What? I saw with my own eyes how you –"

"Once doesn't count!" she interrupted me. "And of course, I only use top-class skin products. I wash my hair with baby shampoo, and then I **rinse** it with **camomile** tea. That magics the particular shine into it."

Johanna was better than anything I could have invented. I wrote like mad and feverishly tried to think of an extra-tricky question. "Is there anything else you study? Have you got any interests?"

"Like what?"

"Something other than beauty and sport."

"Isn't that enough? What sort of thing are you thinking of?"

"Something intellectual. It always goes down well if the reader feels mentally stimulated."

Johanna frowned. "Hmm, I can't think of anything at all off the top of my head ... this is a rather unexpected question."

"You said you were taking your 'A' levels next year," I reminded her. "What's your favourite subject? Languages, or Maths or Art?"

"Art and Music, of course!" cried Johanna. "I sing, too!"

"Well, aren't you incredibly **versatile**! Is there anything you can't do?"

Johanna laughed, flattered. She bent over to me and said in a confidential tone, "I **enrolled for** bal-

---

by the bucketload – in rauen Mengen; to rinse – spülen; camomile – Kamille; versatile – vielseitig; to enroll for – sich anmelden für let lessons. You know, my greatest wish is to be the star of a musical."

"What? A couple of days ago, you said you wanted to study History of Art or Architecture. But maybe I'm **mistaken**."

I knew full well that she had said that. However, she shook her head. "You're mistaken. You're probably mixing me up with somebody else."

I was speechless. "Maybe," I said with difficulty, and stood up. "You've given me lots of material. We'll see whether my paper is interested in the article. Oh, I quite forgot: where are you actually staying?"

"On Sylt? In the *Stadt Hamburg* hotel in Westerland, of course. Where else?"

Of course. Where else. 'Of course' one only has the best address, I thought. "You must be loaded. The *Stadt Hamburg,* your own horse, own stables, ballet lessons, golf ..."

" – and singing lessons," she reminded me. "No need to be jealous, Mimi! Bye, then, that guy's waiting for me."

"Stop, Johanna!"

"What now?"

"I'm writing this piece for my paper back home! Shouldn't I send you the article?"

Johanna hesitated for a moment. "Yes, of course!" she said.

"Then give me your address, okay?"

"Johanna Werner, Raffstraße 13, Wiesbaden. But I have to go now, Mimi!"

I ran back to Carlos and the others.

---

to be mistaken – sich irren

"So, how was she?"

"I don't get it! She speaks three languages, has singing lessons, is learning golf and ballet *and* has her own horse and her own stables! At least that's what she says."

Holly and the boys looked at me in astonishment.

"She lives in Wiesbaden just like you, Constantin."

"She lives in Frankfurt," he corrected me.

"Wiesbaden. Raffstraße 13," I read aloud.

Constantin shook his head. "Did you say Raffstraße? But that's not an 'in' area."

"If I were you, I'd double check that address," said Holly. "Did she tell you where she was staying on Sylt?"

"The *Stadt Hamburg* hotel, Westerland."

Dirk and Kai roared with laughter. "She's staying at Kampen campsite! We even know where her one-man tent is **pitched**. Wow, has she **conned** you!"

"That won't have been her only false account," I **surmised**. "Have any of you got a mobile?"

Constantin reached into his trouser pocket, passed me his, and Holly rattled off the number. Two minutes later we knew for a fact that Johanna was not staying at the *Stadt Hamburg*.

"What a liar!" I snapped my notebook shut and put it in my rucksack. "So what are we going to do now?"

"We're going to the airport to register for the modelling competition," Holly declared promptly.

---

to pitch – aufstellen, aufschlagen;
to con sb – jmdn. betrügen; to surmise – vermuten

"We've discussed it all. The boys are joining in, too."

"You're completely nuts!"

"Of course, we're nuts, but it's worth it for the laugh," asserted Dirk and Kai. "And don't you start acting the spoil-sport, Mimi."

"Don't you have to keep an eye on the beach?"

The pair waved me away. "No problem. Two of our mates will stand in for us."

"Carlos! Constantin! Do you really want to **plunge into** this adventure? Tell me you don't want to!" I pleaded.

"I've always wanted to hit the big time as a male model," Carlos assured me with a **wink**. "Mimi, you're not going to chicken out now, okay?"

---

to plunge into – sich stürzen in; wink – Augenzwinkern

Three kinds of gear?!

Dirk and Kai had their bikes with them too, and so it happened that a few moments later we were riding past Albrecht's little house in the direction of Westerland. Just as we were waiting to turn left at the traffic lights, I remembered that I had left my rucksack next to my chair. "I've got to go back at once!" I cried. "You lot cycle on ahead; I'll catch up with you in a minute!"

"No way, we'll wait for you," they all assured me.

Fortunately, some kind person had put my rucksack on the table so that it was easily visible. Relieved, I quickly checked the contents: pullover, wallet, camera ... so far as I could see, everything was still there. The **proverbial load** fell from my mind; I dashed off, waving and yelling from a distance, "It's all fine!"

The airport is east of Westerland and Wenningstedt and has a turbulent history, as Holly told us.

"In the summer of 1913, the first aeroplane landed there, but it wasn't until the First World War that

---

gear – Sachen; proverbial load – sprichwörtliche Last

bathers and the post were transported – on unstabilized runways. In 1919 the first **scheduled flight** connection opened between Berlin, Hamburg and Sylt, but in 1939 war broke out and the area was converted into a military airfield. For more than 30 years, the airport has only been used for non-military flights."

We had a tail wind and after a good half an hour were standing in front of the airport building, trotting to the information desk.

"We'd like to register for the modelling show on Saturday," declared Holly.

"Then you're in the wrong place," replied the bored woman. "Up the stairs, then left, and down the corridor."

"How far?"

"Sorry?"

"How far along the corridor? To the end?"

"Door's open."

"Are you always this friendly?" asked Holly, unimpressed, and pressed her nose against the glass pane. "We've got such a great island, and you give off such a lousy image. Tut, tut, tut ... If you put all the guests off, we'll have to close all the hotels. You surely realize that, don't you?"

I pulled at Holly's T-shirt. "Come on."

"Just a moment, Mimi." She turned back to the woman behind the window pane. "I want to tell you something: My mother has a guest-house in Wenningstedt. We're dependent on our guests, got it? I'm going to complain about you to my local **MP**.

---

bather – Badegast; scheduled flight – Linienflug;
MP (Member of Parliament) – Abgeordnete/-r

Name?" She pressed her nose flat again so that she could read the writing on the little name-badge that the woman was wearing on her left breast. "Simone Mormann. Fine."

"This is so embarrassing," whispered Constantin close to me.

"I think so, too," Holly agreed loudly. "You **slave away** day and night to satisfy your guests, and then this happens!"

The woman was speechless.

At the top of the stairs, Holly flung her arms around Constantin's neck. "You gave me a great **cue**! That really did for that woman, I reckon."

"I ... you misunderstood me," stammered Constantin. "The way you behaved was what I found embarrassing!"

"I know!" Holly beamed. "But she won't forget my appearance in a hurry."

The blonde woman who was responsible for organizing the party was cool and professional. "Of course, you can still register," she said, and it sounded as if she was pleased to see us. "The fact is that things are moving a bit slowly. So far, we've got one male **entrant** and six female ones; five of them aren't definite yet. You're a welcome addition."

"There's only one male entrant so far?" Constantin repeated in horror.

"You presumably hoped you could make yourself invisible in the crowd, did you?" Kai grinned cheekily. "Not likely. If there are only five people, everyone will be looking at them very closely!"

---

to slave away – schuften; cue – Stichwort;
entrant – Teilnehmer/-in

"I'm **withdrawing** my application," Constantin declared.

"No way. You said yes," Holly **contradicted** him. "Isn't that right, Carlos. You have to keep your promises."

"In general, yes. But this is a special case."

"Crikey, Carlos, I'm relying on your support, and I don't expect you to stab me in the back!" Holly protested.

The blonde cleared her throat. "Could you discuss this later, perhaps?"

"We're already agreed," Holly assured her. "We just need the further information, then we'll push off."

"Not so quickly! You have to fill in the application forms. Do you need something to write with?"

We looked pretty **downcast** at the information that was demanded. "How am I supposed to know my **chest measurement**? Or my waist? I thought only girls had them!" grumbled Kai.

"**Cheating** isn't allowed," the blonde called over to us. "It's true that all measurements will be checked, but if the information you give us doesn't **tally**, the entrant is disqualified!"

Constantin's face **lit up**. He quickly scribbled a couple of lines on the paper and immediately pushed it across the table. "Finished!"

"Not like that, Constantin!" Holly snatched the

---

to withdraw – zurückziehen; to contradict – widersprechen; downcast – niedergeschlagen; chest measurement – Brustumfang; to cheat – mogeln; to tally – übereinstimmen; to light up – sich aufhellen

piece of paper. "Have you got a **centimetre tape measure**? Unfortunately, we left ours at home."

"The **scales** as well?" the blonde wanted to know.

"Yes, unfortunately. You know, they're rather **unwieldy**, and they don't fit into the carriers on our bikes," Holly confessed in a conspiratorial tone. "It's a shame you don't wear a name-badge. Your colleague downstairs –"

"I'm Priska. What else can I do for you?"

"Have you got a weighing scales, or haven't you, Priska?"

Priska laughed, pulled open one of her desk drawers and presented us with an ancient set. "If the weights it shows seem funny, then just **deduct** a couple of kilogrammes," she advised us. "On Saturday, you can always say you **put on weight** without noticing."

"Okay. Mimi, you start."

The given weights were so bizarre that we decided on the following **staggered** arrangement: Holly wrote 49 kilogrammes because we thought that round numbers would look manipulated; I wrote 51; Kai 55; Dirk 57; Carlos 59 and Constantin, who was the tallest of us, wrote 59.5.

We were more precise with the tape measure. "I'm **ticklish**!" yelled Dirk, doubled up with laughter.

Carlos and Constantin remained relatively normal, but Kai paraded around like a **cockerel**, flap-

---

centimetre tape measure – Zentimetermaßband; scales – Waage; unwieldy – unhandlich; to deduct – abziehen; to put on weight – zunehmen; staggered – gestaffelt; ticklish – kitzelig; cockerel – Gockel

ping his arms up and down and crowing, "I'm a party animal, a real party animal, cock-a-doodle-doo!"

"He's completely nuts," Holly remarked, filling the boxes with imaginary figures. "So, Priska, that's it. Now we just need the general information. When should we show up on Saturday? And how? Mimi and me in bikinis and the boys in little **thongs**?"

Constantin turned pale, and Carlos also looked seriously worried.

"I'll organize life-jackets for you," offered Kai. "It's an all-purpose piece; it hides a lack of chest hair, it **disguises** missing muscles, reliably covers all spots, and you always look fully dressed in them. Unfortunately, we only have them in orangey red."

Priska wrinkled her nose. "Hey, aren't you the Baywatch boys from Kampen beach?"

"At last!" Dirk and Kai beamed. "Priska, we made a bet on how long it would take you to recognize us. I reckoned on one minute; my friend and colleague reckoned five. Unfortunately, we both lost; it's taken you a good 20 minutes. Are you a bold little non-swimmer? Scared of water and shy? Allergic to the salt in the sea? Are you afraid of the hopping, biting sand-flies? Why did you only recognize us so late?"

"I go swimming in Westerland," explained Priska, laughing.

"North Sea or the swimming pool?" Dirk immediately asked.

"In summer one, in winter the other."

---

thong – Stringtanga; to disguise – tarnen, verbergen

"Hurrah!" Dirk and Kai clapped their hands together. "You passed the test, Priska. When we –"

"When we've won first prize, we'll invite you to the *Malabar*."

"What if Carlos or Constantin wins first prize?"

"Then Constantin or Carlos will invite you. And us as well, it goes without saying!"

"There's another male entrant," Constantin suddenly said. "What if he nabs first prize?"

"Well, let me worry about that!" Priska laughed. "The boy is my boyfriend. How long do you think it took me to get him to take part in this competition?"

At last, Priska pressed the information sheets into our hands. "If anything changes with you, call this number, okay? And read it all through carefully. You need three kinds of gear to wear. So make sure you don't forget anything important."

"Three kinds of thong?" Holly teased. "Mimi, boys, where are we going to find out about that one?"

"In the *Malabar* – where else? But first of all I'd like to see the hall. Is that okay, Priska?" I asked.

"Sorry, but it's shut. You'll have to wait until 7pm on Saturday."

A dream career!

It had, in fact, been completely stupid to cycle to the *Malabar* at that time of day. As we feared, there wasn't a **spare seat**, so we sat down in the sand.

"So, let's have a closer look at the advert," said Carlos. "Aha, they're looking for male and female talent. What kind of talent?"

"It means you're allowed to demonstrate to the public not only your deluxe body but also your aura," replied Kai. "Could someone tell me how strong my aura is? Do I out-aura you all?"

"Not likely. My aura is stronger than yours!" Dirk **bared his teeth**. "Cheeeeese!"

"It's not enough just to say 'cheese'. Your entire body has to exude aura," said Carlos. "Along these lines!" He stood up, put one leg **graciously** in front of the other and put his hands on his hips. "So, how about it?"

"Ridiculous. You look as if you were a lightweight pretending to be a heavyweight. This is how you do it!" Kai struck a pose and smiled **winsomely**. "That's better, isn't it?"

---

spare seat – freier Platz; to bare your teeth – die Zähne zeigen; gracious – graziös; winsome – gewinnend

"Just a moment." I had read two or three sentences more. "Now I know why they're looking for models. One thing's for sure: it's not about toothpaste."

"Shame!"

"They want someone for a new face-cream."

"Really? What about aftershave?" asked Carlos. "I mean, I've never used cream on my face in my entire life."

"Not even sun lotion?" interrupted Holly.

"I only use soap and water on my skin," said Carlos, quoting a well-known advertising slogan.

"No wonder your face isn't glowing," remarked Dirk. "I use the whole works every day."

"Like what, Dirk?"

"Well, just all the stuff that goes with it!"

"The guy hasn't got a clue!" Holly grinned. "Mimi, what else have you read?"

"Listen, the main point is that the winners and first and second runners-up don't just get taken onto the modelling books – no, they're also invited to a casting in Berlin." I looked at Carlos. "We've never been there. Carlos, we have to win the prizes."

"Okay, you win, and we'll all go together," said Kai. "What are we going to wear on Saturday evening? I have to know. Perhaps I should go on a **spending spree** and buy a new –"

"Don't tell me you've not got a chic thong," teased Holly.

"Hey! Listen to this, you lot! It's one disaster after another!" I cried, lowering the piece of paper. "The dream is over. I've got nothing to wear."

---

spending spree – Großeinkauf

Holly grabbed the piece of paper out of my hands and read, "'At the pre-casting' – eh?"
"**Preliminary** round, that means," Constantin helped her out.
"Okay. 'At the pre-casting, which will start at around 10pm, the competitors are to introduce themselves in casual outfits first of all. Jeans and a T-shirt are what's called for.'" Holly laughed. "Mimi, you can manage that, can't you?"
I nodded, and Holly read on. "'Anyone who isn't convincing in their casual gear is eliminated. In the next round, candidates appear in posh, individual **leisurewear**.'" Holly frowned. "Can anyone tell me what posh, individual leisurewear is? Constantin, surely you know."
"What about a little cashmere pullover with a pearl **necklace** and **ear-studs**? Light reddish-brown Lederhosen would go well with it, or a little flippy skirt made of lightweight silk. On Sylt, a classic, British-inspired twinset wouldn't look wrong, though."
"Blimey, Constantin! Are you in the fashion trade?"
"No." He smirked. "Reading broadens the mind," he laughed. "I like flicking through my mother's **glossy** magazines. I sometimes come across sentences like, for example ..." He closed his eyes and **droned**, "The mini-dress in boxer-style with swinging asymmetric **hem** is made of **poppy**-red silk

---

preliminary – einführend; leisurewear – Freizeitkleidung; necklace – Halskette; ear-stud – Ohrstecker; glossy – Hochglanz-; to drone – herunterleiern; hem – Saum; poppy – Mohnblume

satin with little **perspex hoops** on the **seams**. It has a zip at the front, which absolutely has to be worn open. The outfit is completed by short pink leggings."

"Constantin! You're not remotely as boring as I thought!" cried Holly enthusiastically.

Constantin turned red. "What do you mean? Someone who reads the classics is a loser from the outset, is he?"

"*You* said that," Holly defended herself, holding the piece of paper up to her eyes. She cleared her throat. "'In the final elimination round, the favourites finally have to present themselves –"

"Naked. I thought as much," said Kai.

"Nonsense! ... in a swimsuit or bikini. Thongs are out of the question, and so's naked. So that's that. Have you all got the gear?"

"Jeans, T-shirt and swimsuit aren't a problem. The posh, individual leisurewear does my head in, though. Mimi, we just didn't think of that when we were packing. What a shame," Carlos teased.

"I can lend you a shirt and a matching pair of trousers, Carlos," Constantin said completely unexpectedly. "And my mother's bound to have something for you in her wardrobe, Mimi."

"Wow, that really would be very noble of your mother," said Holly. "The thing is this, Mimi ... I have in fact just got the usual things, jeans and stuff. I'll have to raid my cousin's wardrobe myself, and if she hears that two people want to borrow stuff from her at the same time, she'll have a heart attack."

---

perspex – Acrylglas; hoop – Reifen; seam – Naht

"Then everything's fine. Apart from the most important thing, of course. What awaits the proud winner? Just being added to a model file?"

"Are you a candidate for galloping amnesia? It's the trip to Berlin! We're up for that, aren't we, Mimi?" cried Carlos. "Anyway, being added to the model file would be far too little. Who could prove to us that the file-cards with our names on them wouldn't just land in the wastepaper bin a day later?"

"Absolutely," said Holly, baffled.

"And if they did, the joke's worth it!" Kai helped Dirk up. "Come on, the evening's only just begun. We'll show you the best disco in Westerland."

"Hey, I'm not going to any disco in these clothes," cried Holly.

I agreed with her, **since** without a suitable outfit and make-up, you look seriously old compared to the others.

So we split up at the promenade. Dirk and Kai weren't going to let anything stop them from going to the disco; Constantin cycled to Keitum; Holly to Wenningstedt; and Carlos and I leaned against the wall in front of Sylt's biggest sun-terrace, as they call the promenade, and looked down at the water.

It was still not totally dark, yet the sea was a deep blue. The waves ran onto the beach, white and **sluggish**; the wind carried snippets of conversation and music across to us; and I thought about everything I'd experienced that Thursday. The most important thing was that Carlos and I had cleared up the Schietkram and had made up with one another.

---

since – weil; sluggish – träge

"I'm glad Constantin got over it so quickly," I said quietly.

Carlos pulled me to him. "You're wrong there, Mimi," he replied. "He just doesn't show how hurt he is. It goes against his pride. I wouldn't like to be in his shoes. He feels hellish, no doubt about it." Carlos stroked a **strand** of hair away from my face.

We were standing very close to one another. I could feel his heart beating; I shut my eyes – and when I opened them again, it was dark. Only where sea and sky met was there a streak of shimmering light.

---

strand – Strähne

A nasty surprise

When I came down to the kitchen on Friday morning, Albrecht was already out with Noballs. Märthe was complaining because the sand in the water was bunging up her coffee machine, and there was neither sight nor sound of Carlos.

Yawning, I reached for the Sylt paper, quickly flicked through the political section, skimmed the 'News from North Germany', and **immersed myself in** the island news. On Mondays the people who live in List were allowed to put outside their houses things like clapped-out furniture, defective fridges and used paper for collection. In Morsum, overweight people could exchange their diet stories. In Munkmarsch, people were looking for a lost dog. In Tinnum, there was mother and baby swimming in the mornings and a lecture on Tibet was announced for the evening. A well-known star was staying in Kampen with his current flame and Westerland advised all men that the preferred flirting territory for women wasn't the beach, but the beer garden.

I giggled. "Just listen to this, Marthe: 'The differ-

---

to immerse yourself in – sich vertiefen in

ences between men and women are greater and more dramatic than we thought. Did you know that women prefer to flirt in beer gardens, while men prefer to flirt on the beach? And can you tell me how the two are supposed to come together if the beer garden isn't right in the middle of the beach? We don't know either, and would be very grateful for your tips. Unfortunately, though, beer gardens and beaches aren't the only problem: lots of men don't know how to get a woman to notice them. Forget the flowers and lay a **jellyfish** at a lady's feet? Build her a sandcastle and invite her to it with the words *my home is your castle*? Take part! In the next few days we shall be publishing the most successful tips and tricks on these pages.' Märthe, are you going to take part?"

Märthe laughed. "You know what, Mimi? When I was your age, I'd have been grateful for tricks and tips to keep men at a distance!"

On the next page I spotted an article that gripped me even more. 'Sylt and its people: stories from history' it was headed. It was followed by the story about the man who'd spent his entire life on the sea and had survived all dangers – only to be run over by the Flensburg tram when he was about to enjoy his retirement. Strange coincidence, I thought, that of all stories, this story that I'd recently been told was in today's paper. I frowned, flicked through a bit further – and jumped up. "Märthe!"

"What's the matter?"

"Look, it's Johanna! And this," I skimmed the lines feverishly, "it's exactly what she told me: her

---

jellyfish – Qualle

own stables, own horse, ballet and singing lessons, three languages ... I don't believe it! Two such coincidences on the same day? It's impossible!"

"Let's have a look." Märthe put her glasses on and read under her breath, "'I have a dream: As Johanna tells us, she's taking part in the modelling competition on Saturday. But her greatest dream is to be the star of a musical ...'" So what, Mimi? What have you got against the girl?"

I raced into my room, grabbed my rucksack and opened it with trembling fingers. My notebook! Where was my notebook? My pullover flew out followed by wallet, camera and comb; lipgloss and mascara rolled under the bed – and that was it.

I ran to Carlos and shook him awake. "My notebook's gone, and someone's **knocked up** two articles using my notes!" I cried. "How can you kip for so long! Get up and help me!"

I could barely speak for anger.

"Hey? What? I don't understand," wailed Carlos, struggling out of bed.

"Come into the kitchen and see for yourself!" I ran back downstairs to read the **monstrosities** for a second time.

At that moment the telephone rang. "Hey, Mimi," said Constantin on the other end of the phone. "Have you seen the Sylt paper with Johanna's picture in it?"

"Yes. That wouldn't be so bad on its own. But my notebook's missing. Someone must have stolen it from my rucksack."

---

to knock up – zusammenzimmern;
monstrosity – Gräueltat

"Didn't you check the contents yesterday –"

"Of course, I checked the contents," I interrupted him. "But I was in such a hurry that I didn't notice that the notebook of all things wasn't there any more." I was almost **sobbing**. "Constantin, the whole thing is much worse than you think! Someone has **cobbled together** an article out of the information that Johanna gave me. Did you read the tram story? That was in my notebook, too."

"Really? That really is the limit! What does Carlos say about it?"

"Nothing yet – he's only just got up!" Now I was actually sobbing. "Constantin, what on earth shall I do?"

"Nothing. Can I speak to Carlos?"

"He's still in the bathroom!"

"Okay. I'll be with you in half an hour at the most."

The half hour passed **horrendously** slowly. I could not eat a thing. Albrecht was **conspicuous** by his absence and so was no help. Carlos took the whole thing very calmly, which was no great achievement given that **at the end of the day** it wasn't his notebook. Guaranteed, he'd have got worked up about a newly discovered geological-geomorphological fault. But, unfortunately, it wasn't all about mussels, snails and sea lilies that had died thousands of years ago and were therefore just fossils of no par-

---

to sob – schluchzen; to cobble together – zusammenschustern; horrendous – entsetzlich; conspicuous – auffallend;
at the end of the day – letzten Endes

ticular importance. Here and now it was all about a red-hot **theft**, in which I was the one who had been robbed; I was the one who'd been done out of the fruits of her **well-nigh** week-long island research.

I couldn't **bear** to stay in the same place for a single second longer. When would Carlos have finally finished his breakfast? When would Constantin appear? And why was Albrecht never anywhere to be seen when you needed him most? Who'd **nicked** my notebook? Who was profiting here from my notes? The latter question was the only one I could answer: the person who'd written the two articles. Who was it? I studied the **byline** for the thousandth time: JE. The letters could mean anything! Damn!

"Just have a look and see if JE appears by any other article," said Carlos.

"Good idea! ... No, nowhere else. Only by these two."

However, we did find the **abbreviation** under various articles that had appeared during the last couple of days. We passed this information on to Constantin when he finally came cycling up. **There were no flies on him**; he immediately asked, "Do the articles have anything in common? What I mean is this: are they articles about sporting events, about concerts or exhibitions, about local council meetings?"

"Last week this JE, whoever he or she may be,

---

theft – Diebstahl; well-nigh – beinahe; to bear – ertragen; to nick – klauen; byline – Verfasserzeile; abbreviation – Abkürzung; There were no flies on him. – Ihn legte man nicht so schnell herein.

wrote about a kindergarten summer fête, then a brief report about the 95th birthday of someone called Berni Fichte, then there was the opening of a jewellery shop, and finally the tenth anniversary of a pub. No, it's a real mixture. Wait! The report of the child being saved is also by JE!"

"Then," Constantin **deduced incisively**, "then JE has to be the abbreviation for Jens-UwE."

I felt cross that I hadn't reached this conclusion myself.

"But the question is this: how did JE get hold of Mimi's notebook?" asked Carlos.

"Maybe JE just happened to see me interviewing Johanna, and then stole my notebook when I forgot my rucksack," I said. "Johanna was there with someone else, do you remember?"

"It could also have been a friend or **acquaintance** of JE, who wanted to help him to get a story," said Constantin.

I shook my head, but Constantin persisted. "Why don't you see what's so obvious? Johanna could have stolen the notebook."

"Of course – that's what I thought, Constantin," I said. "But why? Did she write the articles? No way!"

"Why don't you just give the newspaper a ring?" Märthe interrupted, shaking her head. "If things can be done simply, you don't have to complicate matters, do you?"

"Märthe! Why didn't you say so to start with?"

"I thought you three **smart alecs** might work that out for yourselves!"

---

to deduce – erschließen, ableiten; incisive – scharfsinnig; acquaintance – Bekannte/-r; smart alec – Besserwisser/-in

"But we're not ... Carlos, they know you as a life-saver, so you have to ring them," I urged.

We listened expectantly as he asked to speak to Jens-Uwe.

"What's it about? Just about a piece of information. It is in fact a purely private matter. I met Jens-Uwe a couple of days ago and wanted to meet up with him one evening. When will he be in? Not for the rest of the day? Out doing research. Oh, what a shame. Do **pass on regards** from Carlos. Yes, and I'd almost forgotten: who's hiding behind the abbreviation JE? Oh, so that's Jens-Uwe! In particular, the story about the seaman run over by the tram – yes ... Where's he doing his research today? Thanks very much, it can't be helped. Bye!"

"We **gathered**," I said **despondently**.

"Sorry that I couldn't get any further. Jens-Uwe is undoubtedly the writer of the article, but he's out today," said Carlos regretfully.

"Schietkram," I said, **gnashing** my teeth, and heard Noballs barking. "At last!"

"A full house again?" was Albrecht's comment. "No, that's not true, Holly's missing. Probably still making beds and cleaning basins and such like. So what's going on? You all look a bit naffed off?"

We told him what had happened and showed him the newspaper. "Well, you're not exactly the most talented detectives, are you? It's staring you right in the face! Or to put it another way: the answer is being served to us on a plate!"

---

to pass on regards – Grüße ausrichten; to gather – verstehen, mitkriegen; despondent – hoffnungslos; to gnash – knirschen

"What do you mean? Can you explain to us?"

"You'll get there yourselves, I just have to help you on your way a bit."

"Then go on, for goodness' sake!" I cried.

Albrecht was clearly enjoying the whole business. "You say that JE has only written pretty minor pieces thus far."

We nodded.

"Fine. They were reports without photos, weren't they? Today, we find two extensive articles at the same time, with pictures. What does that tell us? It tells us that JE is growing in **significance**. Why? Because JE is **processing** two interesting pieces of information at the same time: one about a pretty girl who wants to make her career on the island, and the other being the tragic account about the death of a seaman. What's more, he's indirectly announcing further articles: 'Stories from History', he calls it. Not bad. JE has made it to his own column; he's making a career with his newspaper."

We waited.

"The best thing about it all is that only we can see a link between the two articles. Can't you see it?"

We shook our heads. "The link is my notebook," I said slowly.

"Well done, Mimi! And what do you deduce from that?"

"He stole it."

"Not necessarily. It could also have got into his hands quite legally."

"Somebody showed JE the notebook and said

---

significance – Bedeutung; to process – aufbereiten

they had found it. JE accepted it **gratefully** because he didn't doubt that what the person was saying was true, and used my notes," I reasoned.

"That could have been how it happened," agreed Albrecht. "So the question is this: who knew about your notebook?"

"Johanna!" we cried.

"Johanna," repeated Albrecht. "Absolutely right. And it's of considerable interest to Johanna for the interview to appear before Saturday. There's no better publicity. The girl is cunning, very cunning. And unscrupulous."

"She certainly is! If only you knew how many lies she'd **doled out** to me! I'm going to find her and demand my notebook back. That wretched creature! She's in for it!"

Albrecht raised a warning hand. "You're in a weak position, Mimi. Have you got a **witness** who can confirm that Johanna opened your rucksack? No, you haven't. So it's your word against hers. It may be that you'd find the book among her things. Where's she staying?"

"At the campsite!"

Albrecht's eyebrows shot up. "Well, then! Although –" he studied Johanna's picture in the paper, "you won't find the notebook in her tent, Mimi. If it were to be there – contrary to all **common sense** – she could, of course, always say that somebody had smuggled it into her tent. But why should anyone do that?" He shrugged his shoulders.

---

grateful – dankbar; to dole out – austeilen;
witness – Zeuge/Zeugin; common sense – Vernunft

I pondered. Then I stood up. "Right then, Albrecht. Jens-Uwe is out somewhere on the island, so we're not likely to find him. So let's begin our search with Johanna, even if we can assume that we'll not find my precious notebook in her tent. Can I borrow Noballs?"

Albrecht nodded **understandingly**. "Of course, you can. If I were you, I'd take him, too."

"Why? What for?" asked Carlos, confused.

"To find Johanna's tent. To shock her, if she happens to be there," replied Constantin with a grin.

"You see? I just had to help you on your way a bit," said Albrecht laughing. "Don't forget that dogs have to be on leads on Sylt, okay?"

---

understanding – verständnisvoll

Freedom for Noballs!

On foot, you can cover the distance from Sjipwai to the campsite in just a few minutes, especially when you can't walk fast enough for a happily barking Noballs. We were already standing at the entrance to the campsite when Constantin suddenly held Carlos and me back. "There are two possibilities," he said frowning. "Either we can ask here where Johanna's tent is, or we can ask Kai and Dirk first. If you ask me – I'd choose the second option."

"Why make it so complicated?" I protested. "We'll be seen whatever. And I bet there will be loads of people who'll be able to describe us exactly later on."

"What if Johanna's in her tent?"

"All the better," I said, full of **belligerence**. "That's exactly what I want."

Carlos hesitated. "I'd rather **approach** this cautiously," he said, and Constantin agreed with him. "Look, Mimi, it's just a matter of a few minutes' delay. Come on. We'll ask Kai and Dirk, then we'll

---

belligerence – Kampfeslust; to approach sth – an etwas herangehen

creep up to the tent. The more information we have, the better."

Reluctantly, I gave in. Fortunately, the sea was calm. There was a gentle breeze, but neither the **swell** nor an unexpected monster was threatening the bathers – which meant that Kai and Dirk were **loafing around**, bored, outside their little red hut, and were delighted to see us. They went into great detail about their **conquests** at the disco, and finally wanted to know whether we'd got together our gear for the catwalk yet.

"We've still got to sort that," explained Constantin. "What we wanted to ask you was this: have you seen Johanna today?"

"Yes, in the papers!" The pair laughed. "Mimi, someone beat you to it. What bad luck!"

I nodded and said coolly. "What bad luck? What's bad luck is that someone stole my notes and used them to cobble together an article. What do you think to that?"

"Come on, that can't be true!"

"But it is true," said Carlos. "Of course, we're wondering who stole Mimi's notebook. It can only be ..."

"The fact is," I interrupted him, "the fact is that I forgot my rucksack yesterday in the *Silberkanne* garden. You know that much. When I went to fetch it, it wasn't next to the table we were sitting at, but *on* it. Of course, I opened it up and checked that everything was still in it – but I didn't check it closely enough. I remember seeing the pullover right at

---

swell – Wogen; to loaf around – faulenzen; conquest – Eroberung

the top. In fact, the book should have been at the top, but it could well have slipped down inside, or so I thought. It wasn't until this morning, when I'd read the paper, that I noticed it was missing."

The pair had listened attentively. "That's a damned stupid story," said Kai. "What are you going to do? Go to the police?"

Noballs **tugged** at the lead.

"Course not. Who will have seen someone opening a strange rucksack and making off with a little black book?"

"Have you already been to the *Silberkanne*?"

"No. We wanted to talk to Johanna first; maybe she knows something," replied Constantin. "Could you tell us where her tent is?"

"Of course." Dirk and Kai readily described Johanna's **accommodation** to us. "You can't miss it. For one thing, it's deep blue; for another, it's pretty old – I reckon she bought it second-hand or just borrowed it. For a third thing, there are no table or chairs outside it; and fourthly and most strikingly, she's tied a yellow cloth to the **tent pole**."

Kai **poked** Dirk in the ribs and mimicked Johanna's voice: "You'll find me with no difficulty because I've put up a marker: a little handkerchief is fluttering in the breeze. It's yellow, like the sun, and says: Johanna lives here!"

"Thanks very much for the information!"

"Who's the mutt you've got on the lead, Mimi?" Kai wanted to know.

"That's Noballs. Guys, I hope you have more luck

---

to tug – ziehen; accommodation – Unterkunft; tent pole – Zeltstange; to poke – stoßen than the dog!" I said, entertaining those present with Noballs' story.

The pair of them sympathized wholeheartedly with Noballs, and made us promise to return after the campsite operation, come what may.

So we set off and were soon **strolling** through the passageways between the camper trucks and large and small tents. Even from a distance we could see the yellow cloth. It was fluttering cheerfully in the breeze.

"The zip's shut," I murmured. "Either she's still asleep, or she's gone out. Let's get stuck in!"

Now Noballs had to play his role and create **havoc**. The many unusual, promising smells aroused his curiosity; the lead slipped through my fingers – quite **unintentionally**, of course! – and he shot off. "Stop him!" the boys yelled. "Bello, come back! Come back at once!"

Noballs didn't listen to the name 'Bello'. He ran and ran, knocking over a chair here and barely missing a table there; we stumbled over **tent pegs** and ropes, crying 'Bello' at the tops of our voices.

Noballs kept stopping to look at us. His eyes were shining, and he had an expression on his face that made it seem as if he knew full well that it was all just a great joke. If we almost caught him, he'd then run off again, barking. Fortunately, there were three of us. We finally managed to drive him in the right direction and, what's more, quite a few people had joined in the **chase** in the meantime.

---

to stroll – spazieren, bummeln; havoc – Chaos; unintentional – unbeabsichtigt; tent peg – Zeltpflock, Hering; chase – Jagd

Noballs ran towards Johanna's tent. I stumbled over a tent peg, fell, held tightly to a rope, and pulled the foremost tent peg out of the sand. With two quick movements, I also pulled out the middle and back ones and pulled hard on the rope; the tent tilted and tipped on one side. No sound came from within, so Johanna wasn't there.

"Got him!" yelled Carlos.

"Hanna, have you cut your knee?" Constantin bent over me **anxiously** and helped me up.

"Yes, and it hurts," I wailed. My performance was so convincing that a man immediately offered to fetch a plaster.

"No, no, that's really not necessary," I protested. "But the tent – it's terrible that the tent has almost collapsed!"

"You keep hold of the dog," Constantin said to Carlos. "We'll put the tent back up. If you open the zip, Hanna, and hold up the topmost tent pole, I'll bang the pegs back in and **tighten** the ropes." Constantin took off one of his shoes.

"I'll fetch you my **rubber mallet**," said one of the **bystanders**. "Who wants to ruin his shoes?"

"That's very kind of you," Constantin said **approvingly**.

While the helpful person went to fetch the rubber mallet, I crept into the tent. I almost had a heart attack: I'd expected anything, total chaos, clothing lying around everywhere, a crumpled up sleeping bag, dirty crockery and more besides. But I hadn't

---

anxious – besorgt; to tighten – straffen; rubber mallet – Gummihammer; bystander – Zuschauer/-in; approving – zustimmend

even dreamt of such order: everything was **immaculately** tidy! The sleeping bag was neatly arranged and plumped up; a big **holdall** stood at the head end; four hangers with various items of clothing hung on the pole; and what made the whole thing so laughable was the big white candle in a **preserving jar**. The poor girl couldn't even afford a decent camping lantern!

I opened the holdall and checked through the contents. My notebook wasn't inside, but I did find a plastic bag underneath the holdall. Damn: it just contained several carefully folded T-shirts which were presumably supposed to be ironed out by the weight of the holdall.

I sat back on my **heels** and looked around. Where would I hide stolen goods? Of course: in the sleeping bag!

I was just unzipping it when I heard a man asking outside, "Is the girl in the tent?"

"How are you getting on? Can I hold the pole up yet?" I quickly called.

"Just wait a moment, Hanna," Constantin replied from outside. "The ropes are tangled!"

I wondered why on earth the guy had managed to come up with the name Hanna. But it was clever of him not to use my or Noballs' real names, really it was!

Regardless of whether it was true that the ropes were in a tangle or whether Constantin wanted to play for time, I put my hand into the sleeping bag. Empty. But – I **rejoiced** silently: on the outside was

---

immaculate – untadelig; holdall – Reisetasche; preserving jar – Einmachglas; heel – Ferse; to rejoice – sich freuen

a small **rectangular** pocket in which there was a lighter, an open packet of cigarettes and – my notebook!

"I'm done!" I cried, trying to suppress the excitement in my voice.

"Okay, then push the pole up!"

I could hear a couple of **muffled thumps** and Noballs' excited barking. "Everything's fine! You can come out!"

I crept outside, smoothed my hair and carefully shut the zip again.

"You see, that's the reason I don't stay in a hotel," said the helpful man in **tracksuit bottoms** and a vest. "There's always something going on at a campsite!"

---

rectangular – rechteckig; muffled – gedämpft;
thump – Schlag; tracksuit bottom – Trainingshose

The notebook and the net stockings

We were barely out of sight when Carlos asked, "So tell us, Mimi, where and how did you find the book?"

"Did you get a look in the tent? Then let me tell you that Johanna's the tidiest person you could ever imagine. There's nothing lying around; everything's scrupulously clean. Not even my aunts are that **painstaking**!"

"That does sound very uncomfortable, but it must have made your search easier, mustn't it?" asked Constantin.

"Precisely." By the time I'd recounted exactly what it looked like in Johanna's tent and what was in the little pocket of the sleeping bag, we were standing outside the red Baywatch-hut.

"Well?" Kai asked **eagerly**.

I waved my notebook triumphantly.

"Ten euros," said Kai to Dirk, holding out his hand. Dirk wailed, "Can't we spend the money together? Who likes losing ten whole euros?"

It turned out that the pair of them had had a bet

---

net stockings – Netzstrümpfe; painstaking – gewissenhaft, sorgfältig; eager – begierig

about whether or not Johanna had stolen the notebook and hidden it in her tent.

"Boys, I'll put down another ten euros, then we can celebrate together this evening," suggested Constantin.

"Have you got that much cash?" asked Kai.

"Nothing to do with you," Dirk **rebuked** him. "Main thing is, he **coughs up the dough**! So tell us what happened!"

We tied Noballs to the hut and threw ourselves down on the sand. The sun was baking; the sea lay unusually calm at our feet; and Kai passed a can of cola around.

"There's one thing I just don't understand," said Dirk. "Imagine I were to steal something. I'd be intending to pass this something on to someone else so that the someone else could also make use of it. Now I ask you this: why should I want to have the something back afterwards? It would be an unnecessary **burden**, wouldn't it? And on top of that, as in this case, a **piece of evidence**? No, guys, that doesn't make sense."

Constantin brushed his hair off his forehead with his characteristic gesture. "Admittedly, Johanna's way of acting is a complete mystery to me. Let's say she saw Mimi's rucksack and opened it. What did she find inside? She's got her own comb and lipstick. What about the pullover, Mimi?"

"Old, well-worn and only fit for emergencies," I said briefly and **succinctly**.

---

to rebuke sb – jmdn. tadeln; to cough up the dough – die Moneten herausrücken; burden – Last; piece of evidence – Beweisstück; succinct – knapp

"The camera?"

"If only she'd stolen that or my money!" I rolled my eyes. "Unthinkable!"

"She didn't take valuables like money or the camera," Constantin continued. "She stole the notebook, passed the information on to Jens-Uwe, but kept the book. Why? There must be a very specific reason for that."

"Well, yes, but what?"

"Real adventures happen in the mind," I quoted. "I bet we'll find out why Johanna did it like this rather than any other way."

"Ten euros?" Dirk held his hand out to me.

We laughed. Noballs barked. I stood up to throw the empty can in the litter-bin, and discovered the reason for Noballs' delight: Holly and Albrecht!

The two of them were tramping towards us.

"Holly thought we'd be bound to find you here," cried Albrecht, **fending off** Noballs, who was trying to jump up him. "So, how did it go?"

"Brilliant!"

"Why didn't you wait for me?" asked Holly. "I'm so cross with you!"

"I was much too angry to wait for you to finish cleaning all your wash-basins and polishing the floors," I replied, and told her about the successful recapture of my notebook. "Now I'm going to find Johanna and make her explain herself. She's really **got it coming to her**!"

"What do you expect to **gain** by that?" asked Albrecht.

---

to fend off – abwehren; She's got it coming to her. – Die kann was erleben.; to gain – gewinnen, erreichen

"What a question! Am I supposed to act as if nothing's happened?"

"Just consider the matter with a clear head," Albrecht said. "You can't prove that she took the notebook out of the rucksack that you had forgotten. But lots of people saw that you were in her tent. What if she says you'd stolen something valuable? Jewellery for example?"

"But that's nonsense! I'll hold the notebook under her nose and ..."

"... she'll say she's never seen it before."

"Then I'll say that it was in the pocket of her sleeping bag."

"So? Who can prove that you didn't hide it there yourself? Or, even more straightforwardly, that it never was in her tent, but that you brought it with you and made up a story to **blacken** her name? No, Mimi, **the cards** really **are not stacked in your favour**. But there's something else," continued Albrecht. "Holly told me that you all want to take part in this **insane** modelling competition."

We nodded.

"The fact is, Johanna applied long before you. What if she says you're **pinning** a theft **on** her that she never committed, to make her look bad in public? So much so that she's forced to withdraw from the competition? Nobody wants to have a thief in their midst, Mimi."

"How does she know that we've applied?" I cried. "All I want is –"

---

to blacken – beschmutzen; The cards are not stacked in your favour. – Du hast keine Chance.; insane – wahnsinnig; to pin sth on sb – jmdm. etwas anhängen

Carlos put his hand on my arm. "What Albrecht's trying to tell you, Mimi, is that you should let the matter rest. You've got your notebook back; you're writing the article for the *Daily Post*, in any case; and you should forget what happened here as quickly as possible."

I shook my head **stubbornly**. "What Johanna did was wrong. I want to prove it to her."

"Why? She knows it herself. Maybe she feels really lousy and wishes the whole thing had never happened," Kai threw in.

"Her?" I **snorted**. "She only thinks about what's good for *her* and what *she* gets out of it!"

"I reckon Johanna is exactly as Mimi says," Constantin said unexpectedly yet very firmly. "She couldn't care less if we see through her. Self-doubt and reflection on her own character don't figure."

"Crikey, Constantin!" said Holly, almost **in awe**. "Where have you got that from?"

"He reads," Albrecht answered for him. "Everyone only has a certain number of experiences during his life. That's the way it should be. But it's also good to know about more than you actually experience. And that's what reading does for you."

Constantin nodded. "That's right." He looked at the time and said, "Mimi, I told my mother about our insane plan and that you didn't have any posh, individual leisurewear with you. She'd be delighted if you'd come to see her this afternoon. Maybe you'll find something suitable."

"Oh!" On the one hand, I had long since written

---

stubborn – dickköpfig; to snort – schnauben;
in awe – ehrfürchtig

off the idea of a posh yet completely outdated twinset, and had finally reconciled myself with difficulty to the idea of buying the **requisite** little skirt – **cropped**, of course. On the other hand, I liked his mother and particularly the story of her twentieth birthday. Carlos and I had established that she had evidently been a real Wanda back then. It was possible that she'd tell me today what had made her change.

"Are you coming, Carlos? To try on your costume?"

He screwed up his nose. "That's asking a bit much, Mimi. I'd rather stay with Kai and Dirk and play at Baywatch. **Provided** you remember about the Schietkram!"

"Done!"

"Don't be late," Albrecht asked me. "I've invited an old friend especially for you, who'll be able to tell you all sorts of things about the island."

"Fine! Bye!"

As I walked to the bikes with Constantin, I screwed up all my courage. "Constantin, are you still cross with me?"

He turned red. "Cross is completely the wrong word," he murmured. "I'm sad because I feel so helpless."

"Helpless?" I repeated, confused. "I don't understand."

"No?" He smiled, but the smile wasn't in the slightest bit happy. "Life **punishes** the latecomers. Unfortunately, I was a latecomer. You belong to

---

requisite – erforderlich; cropped – *hier:* kurz;
provided – vorausgesetzt; to punish – bestrafen

Carlos, and there's nothing that can be done about it. Full stop." He raised his shoulders. "I can **cope with** it, Mimi, don't worry about that. It'll take a while, it hurts, and when I see you or stand near to you or when your hair blows into my face, as it's doing now, I'd love to take you in my arms."

His face turned even redder as he said, "I've always dreamt of a girl like you."

"What am I supposed to be like, then?"

"You don't do what everyone else does. You've chosen your own path. What other girl of your age is already **freelance** for a newspaper? I admire that about you. But that's by no means everything ..."

"Constantin, stop exaggerating!" Resolutely, I pushed my bicycle onwards. "I hope you meet a much nicer girl than I am."

"Thanks!"

"You're welcome!" I held my hand out to him. "Everything okay?"

He hesitated. "Will you write to me?"

"Of course! And when I'm travelling, I'll send you a particularly nice postcard!"

We cycled to Keitum. Constantin's mother was sunbathing by the pool and was glad to have company. She and Constantin were staying in an apartment: two bedrooms and a living room – seriously posh!

Unfortunately, her clothes were a flop, nothing but silk blouses and twinsets, completely useless from a modelling point of view. "How about a shopping trip to Keitum?" she asked.

---

to cope with sth – mit etwas klarkommen;
freelance – selbstständige/-r Mitarbeiter/-in

"Mum! Westerland would definitely be more suitable," cried Constantin. "Think how old we are!"

Susanne – I had long since been calling her by her first name – saw me hesitating. "A shopping trip is fine, but I'll pay for my own things," I said firmly.

"Of course! What else did you think?" she said, laughing. "I'll help you to choose the right thing, and if it works out a bit more expensive, I'll help you out, okay?"

"It simply can't work out a bit more expensive!"

Susanne had a car which took us to Westerland in no time at all.

In the first boutique there was nothing but **hideous**-looking **rags**. In the second, we found a thin skirt with **flounces** and a top to match. It looked good on the hangers, but I felt terribly overdressed in it. In the third shop, right at the back of the **rail**, we discovered a red and white striped mini-skirt and socks with the same stripes.

"Not bad," was Susanne's opinion. We **rooted around** in the pullovers and **cardigans**. "Look, this colour is fab!" It was a little dark green shirt with **frayed** seams, and it went perfectly with the skirt and the socks. Unfortunately, the whole lot was pretty expensive. Damn: should I or shouldn't I? I bought the outfit. It was just too much of a pity to leave it for someone else. After that, I was bankrupt.

"What about shoes?" asked Susanne, pulling me across the street.

---

hideous – scheußlich; rag – Fetzen; flounce – Volant; rail – Kleiderstange; to root around – herumwühlen; cardigan – Wolljacke; frayed – ausgefranst

"I've got shoes," I said firmly.

"Fine, if you're sure. Otherwise I'd – Mimi, just look at that! That would be the ultimate eye-catcher, wouldn't it?"

The girl on the advertising **hoarding** was wearing a mini-skirt similar to the one I'd bought, and socks to match – but the really great thing about it was that she was wearing net stockings underneath.

"I'll buy you those net stockings!" Susanne was off on one. "Not a word against it, I'm paying!"

"Why are you doing all this, Susanne? You don't know me, and you'll presumably never see me again, so why?"

She stopped and looked at me. Really seriously and thoughtfully and sharply, and in such a way that I knew that it was important for her to tell me the truth rather than just saying whatever came into her head.

"I can't answer that question in one quick sentence. I think we'll buy the stockings first, then we'll sit somewhere where we won't be disturbed."

"Great," said Constantin. "I need to get something else, too. Where shall we meet? In the bistro?"

We agreed on a time and pushed off. It was difficult to find net stockings with extra-large holes like the ones the girl was wearing in the advert, but we **struck lucky**!

Later, in the bistro, Susanne immediately ordered tea for us both, but then asked in horror, "Oh my goodness, might you prefer something else? That funny milky coffee for instance?"

---

hoarding – Tafel; to strike lucky – Glück haben

"No, tea is fine. So, why have you sacrificed your afternoon and bought me stockings as well?" I asked without further ado. "When I've been so **rotten to** Constantin!" I pulled a face.

It took a while for her to get going. "Constantin told me everything. Well, I reckon things really haven't gone that well between you," she affirmed. "But didn't you have to work out what your own feelings really were first?"

I nodded.

"There you go. You and Constantin had a wonderful evening, but when you met the next day, you didn't make any **pretence**. You told him the truth and said that it was your mistake and that you were sorry – and that was the end of the matter so far as you were concerned. I think that was good."

"And Constantin?"

"He's suffering, of course he is, but he can't just tell his feelings how to behave. And anyway, to be very honest, Mimi, holiday romances don't last. Most people want a couple of nice days, then they part and go home with their memories."

"True."

"Have you already had that experience?"

"I visited my sister in Hong Kong – she worked there as an au-pair after her A' levels. I met a boy there who I thought was the love of my life. Just before we were about to meet in Paris, he e-mailed to say it was all over. Just like that, with no reason. After that, I was never going to fall in love again."

---

to be rotten to sb – zu jmdm. gemein sein;
pretence – Ausrede

Susanne smiled. "No doubt you could have done without that experience, eh?"

"Of course. My aunts **prescribed** a trip to Chile to make me feel better. That's where I met Carlos. He was also suffering from serious love-sickness at the time, and wanted to use me to get revenge on his ex-girlfriend. Oh well, I realized that his motives weren't the most noble, and was seriously angry. But at some point, something just clicked after all."

"How did Carlos get from Chile to Germany?"

I told Susanne that he was studying near my home town of Stuttgart, and that we had already been travelling together several times. "But we almost split up in Morocco!" I had actually been intending to quiz Susanne, but somehow it came about that I was doing all the talking. Even the business with Wanda and the fact that we'd called her, Susanne, Wanda as well.

"But now you're not a Wanda at all," I stated. "How come?"

"Wanda! I like it!" Susanne ordered another tea. "I was in fact a Wanda, but I think that kind of trying-out phase is part of life. If you don't have it at the right time, you have to make up for it later, and then you often can't get out of it. That's how it was for my husband, who was the male version of a Wanda – and stayed that way. The time with him wasn't easy but I survived."

"How?"

Susanne laughed. "Someone once told me a really stupid saying: 'If life gives you a lemon, turn it into lemonade.' I **stuck to** that and thought that

---

to prescribe – verordnen; to stick to – sich halten an

lemonade was better and above all less boring than water."

"I'll make a note of that saying!" I hesitated. "Constantin told us that his father only died very recently."

"That's true," replied Susanne, but didn't **pursue** that one. Instead, she asked for more information about Wanda.

"The Wanda we knew was a real good-for-nothing cow. She had to prove to every man how fantastic and **irresistible** she was, regardless of whether he had a girlfriend or not."

"I know all about that." Susanne laughed. "That's what some people are like. The problem is bearing with them if you're not like that yourself. I have a female friend who's a real Wanda. She's with a man who's just the same. It works."

"No!"

"Yes it does, but it wouldn't work for me."

"Self-doubt and reflection on her own character don't figure," I **recalled**.

"Sorry?"

"That's what Constantin said."

"Was he talking about his father?"

"No, no, we were just talking generally about Johannas and Wandas." Aha, so that was it. Constantin's father had been a male Wanda. And not only his mother, but also Constantin himself had suffered from this.

"Are you coming to the modelling competition, Susanne?"

---

to pursue sth – auf etwas weiter eingehen; irresistible – unwiderstehlich; to recall – sich erinnern

"Maybe. I don't know yet."

"Johanna's going to win."

"I'm not so sure," said Susanne. "However, it does depend on what type they're looking for: the tall blonde, the exotic look, or someone like you. It'll be exciting whatever."

I grinned. "Especially because the boys are joining in!"

Whaling story and Egg King

By now, it was so late that Susanne took me back to Kampen in the car, and Constantin promised to bring my bike over the next day.

Albrecht was already sitting in the front room with his friend Wulf Martin and Carlos.

"Here you are at last," said Carlos. I could clearly read in his eyes: *Have you been causing Schietkram*?

I shook my head and gave him a quick kiss. "Unfortunately, I had to buy some suitable clothes after all. Susanne's selection was just too posh and therefore completely unsuitable. Shall I show you what I've bought?"

The men laughed. "We'll see you tomorrow evening in it, in any case," said Albrecht. "Wulf Martin and I aren't going to miss the spectacle."

"Does that mean you're coming, too?"

"Yes, and Märthe," affirmed Albrecht. "She'll sort us out with **ear-plugs** because she reckons your noisy music is too loud for our delicate ears and will resound across the whole island."

"Ear-plugs are good. And don't forget your binoculars; the party hall is massive."

---

ear-plug – Ohrstöpsel

"Will do. Look here, Wulf Martin has brought you something." He pointed at a rope that was twisted into a **noose**.

"What's that?" I asked. "A noose with a history or something? Did it once hang from a **gallows**?"

Wulf Martin snorted. "Nothing of the sort! Albrecht wants me to tell you a bit about the island. This thing here belongs to its history like whaling or the Egg King."

What, for goodness' sake, was an Egg King? Carlos raised his eyebrows and I opened the notebook I'd stolen back.

"Ropes," began Wulf Martin, running his **specimen** through his **gnarled** fingers, "were made on the mainland out of **hemp**. Here on the island, we couldn't grow **flax** as the climate wasn't suitable. But we did need ropes."

"For washing lines?"

"Yes, that too, although there wasn't much demand for them. Ships' ropes were more important, as well as ropes to **secure** the sails. But just as important were the ropes for roofs."

"For roofs?" I repeated uncomprehendingly.

"So what were ropes made of on the island? And how?" asked Carlos.

"As I said, we couldn't grow flax. But on the island we have grasses like **sand rye**. The **stalks** were cut down in summer and dried out until winter. In this state they were **brittle** and inflexible, so they

---

noose – Schlinge; gallows – Galgen; specimen – Exemplar; gnarled – knotig; hemp – Hanf; flax – Flachs; to secure – sichern; sand rye – Strandroggen; stalk – Stängel, Halm; brittle – spröde

were put in water and then, when they had turned soft, they were firstly knocked flat with a mallet and finally rubbed between the palms of the hands until they were round. On one day, a capable rope-maker could make a rope of around 100 metres long."

"He rubbed the malleted stalks between his bare hands? The man presumably didn't have very gentle hands then?"

Albrecht laughed loudly and Wulf Martin raised his paw. "Rope-makers didn't give that sort of thing a second thought. The work was hard and demanded a quite particular skill. Moreover, it also brought something in: a 100-metre-long rope represented, after all, the value of half a **hundredweight** of **grain**. Making ropes was often the only source of income for island **dwellers** who were too poor to become professional fishermen."

"Was that in the Middle Ages?" asked Carlos.

"Whatever are you thinking of! Things were like that until into the 20th century!" explained Wulf Martin. "And now we come to the roofs. Lots of ropes were needed to bind the bundles of **thatch** together and to sew them to the **slats** with a needle as thick as your finger. Nowadays people use wire – don't ask your doctor or chemist about the side effects of this: ask the fire brigade!"

Albrecht confirmed this with a nod. "You can imagine that a thatched roof could dry out and go up in flames in no time at all **due to** a flash of lightning or **negligence**, especially in summer if it

---

hundredweight – Zentner; grain – Korn;
dweller – Bewohner/-in; thatch – Stroh; slat – Latte;
due to – wegen; negligence – Nachlässigkeit

hadn't rained for a while. They didn't put up a whole load of **lightning conductors**. They always had a long pole with a bent iron **hook** as well, ready for emergencies. This was used to tear the bundles of thatch, which were burning like **tinder**, from the roof, and so contain most of the damage. Nowadays, the thatch can't be pulled down so easily because they use wire to bind and secure it. So everything has its advantages and disadvantages."

"On the other hand, the wire presumably lasts much longer," I suggested.

"The thatch lasts an incredibly long time," replied Wulf Martin.

"But there's another important thing: sand rye stops the sand of the dunes from moving. Therefore from the 19th century onwards, you had to have special permission from a beach inspector if you wanted to cut them down."

I had made a note of the key words. "Thrilling. I'll look at the roofs with great respect in future. But who, please, was the Egg King?"

"*What* was an Egg King," Wulf Martin corrected me. "To answer this question, we have to go back into the island's history again and take account of its special features. Well, back then, gulls and geese nested on the island. Their breeding ground was **leased**, and the landlords were entitled to collect and sell a certain proportion of the eggs. A gull's egg was worth around three hen's eggs, and the whole **yield** could **amount to** as much as 70,000 eggs in a

---

lightning conductor – Blitzableiter; hook – Haken; tinder – Zunder; to lease – pachten; yield – Ertrag, Ausbeute; to amount to – sich belaufen auf

season – which, of course, spurred on unauthorized egg-**harvesters** or egg thieves. To stop them stealing, the landlords chose an Egg King, who lived in his egg-hut and guarded the territory. A further characteristic of the island often made his work difficult, but helped the egg thieves quite unfairly; our **notorious** sea-mists **shroud** everything so quickly in cloud in a way that you normally find only in the mountains."

"And they're the reason why you should never go into the tidal flats alone and as a stranger," added Albrecht. "Are we boring you?"

"No!" Carlos and I cried together, and I protested, "Not at all! So the Sylt people traded in thatch and birds' eggs. There was also fish, and mussels, and what else?"

"Oysters, sheep's wool and salt," added Albrecht.

"Oh, the 'white gold'!" Wulf Martin had talked himself into a state of enthusiasm. "That's a story in itself! There are so many bits to it that I'd need a whole evening to tell you everything."

"The most important things **in brief**," requested Albrecht.

"I'll try," declared Wulf Martin. "You know that people need salt to live. That applied to the Sylt people in good times as in bad – but I'll **proceed** one step at a time. Salt was gained by people cutting **peat** in the tidal flats at low tide. This was burnt, and the remaining salt was cleaned in gigantic pots. So far, so good. People used this to **season** their

---

harvester – Erntehelfer/-in; notorious – berüchtigt; to shroud – verhüllen; in brief – kurz und bündig; to proceed – weitermachen; peat – Torf; to season – würzen

food, to salt meat and fish – herrings mostly – and thereby gained markets that were further away and sold the **surplus**. Well, there are two sides to every coin. You know the good side, now comes the bad. I said that the salt-**drenched** peat was cut. What that actually meant was that a lot of the land wasted away, and as a result, whole areas of the island were made lower than they had been. And in conjunction with storm tides, the end result was catastrophic **losses** of land. So the 'white gold' was both blessed and cursed. Have I told you enough now?"

"There's still the whaling story," I reminded him.

"Mimi is **insatiable**," wailed Wulf Martin innocently. "Now she wants to know how the men went whaling!"

"You were the one who mentioned the story," Albrecht reminded him.

"Well, then! Now, do you land-lubbers know that there were in fact up to 5,000 ships in the whaling **stretch** of waters during the summer months? And that a whale-catching ship was barely any longer than a whale?"

No, of course, we hadn't known that. I wrote as he spoke and could hardly keep up.

"A fully-grown animal measures between 30 and 40 metres. The men changed over to smaller boats, the so-called gigs, and if you can picture the relative sizes, that alone will tell you how risky the whole business was. But when you realise that they had to attack the whale directly from in front or behind –

---

surplus – Überschuss; drenched – durchzogen, durchnässt; loss – Verlust; insatiable – unersättlich; stretch – Ausdehnung from the blind spot, in other words – this meant that it was absolutely necessary to get as close to it as five to ten metres. In this way they could hit the whale with the harpoon. You can imagine how much courage they needed to do it. Courage, skill and experience were all demanded – and **a good deal of luck**. The harpoon didn't kill the creature. But if it was sitting firmly in the layer of **blubber**, then that's when the hunt really began. Then it could happen that the whale shook off the harpoon. Or he dived vertically down into the sea. Or, and this was the most dangerous possibility, he pulled the gig and its crew under the ice if the **mooring** rope wasn't cut in time. But if everything went well and the whale was finally exhausted, then a deadly blow was **inflicted** on him with a lance. Then it was straight on with the next bit of work. The animal was **dissected** bit by bit. The strips of blubber were put into barrels and gave around 17,000 litres of **train-oil** per animal, which was used to light the lamps and street-lanterns. The strong and highly flexible **baleen**, or whalebone, was used to make buttons, combs, **hair slides**, corsets and goodness knows what else."

"Don't forget the **rods** and poles for parasols and umbrellas," Albrecht added.

"That's right. We, Albrecht and I, can still clearly remember the **fish liver oil** that we had to swallow

---

a good deal of luck – eine ganze Menge Glück; blubber – Walfischspeck; to moor – vertäuen, festmachen; to inflict – zufügen; to dissect – zerteilen, sezieren; train-oil – Fischtran; baleen – Barte; hair slide – Haarspange; rod – Stange; fish liver oil – Lebertran

after the war, and which tasted simply disgusting. The whalebones served as substitute posts on the island, since we don't have any forests, and also as beams. And finally we mustn't forget that there were also artists who **carved** entire whaling stories into the bones."

"To make them easily visible, the hollows were coloured black with ash," added Albrecht. "You could admire several examples of this in the local museum, if you had a bit of time spare. By the way, whaling created jobs that have long since died out now: there weren't just seamen, **boatswains** and **helmsmen**, but also harpooners and **blubber-slicers**."

Wulf Martin nodded. "Nor must we forget the wives of the whalers, who looked after house and home during the summer months and had to manage independently. When the man – God willing – came home in autumn, he took over again, which the women, of course, didn't find easy, and which could lead to some pretty turbulent marriages." He smiled. "No, Mimi, I don't know any stories about that. Anyway, I've talked enough for now. Albrecht shouldn't act as though he didn't know anything. Ask *him* if there's anything else you're interested in." He hauled himself out of the armchair with difficulty. He rubbed his back and said that getting old was a real Schietkram.

"Everything has its advantages and its disadvantages," said Carlos, laughing, and helped him into his jacket.

---

to carve – schnitzen; boatswain – Bootsmann;
helmsman – Steuermann; blubber-slicer – Speckschneider

"True, my boy. But there's always an exception to every rule – let me tell you, old age is precisely this exception."

We accompanied him to the door, thanked him and said goodbye. He made me promise to send him a copy of my article, then set off for home.

"Well, Mimi, have you got enough of a haul of Sylt stories now?" asked Albrecht, yawning widely. "My God, it's already almost midnight. Time for bed. I bet Holly will be on the doormat first thing tomorrow, ringing the bell like mad and calling, 'It's the big day!' You've presumably not seen or heard anything more of this Johanna?"

The clock, which was also one of the island's peculiarities because one half of it was in the corridor and the other half in the front room, **for thrift's sake**, prepared to strike. There was a rattling that sounded like somebody with a serious smoker's cough taking a deep breath. We counted along with it. On exactly the twelfth stroke, the doorbell rang.

"Holly! The big day has arrived!" cried Carlos.

Albrecht was at the door in two **strides**. "Fire? Attack? Come in, Detective Superintendent!"

"Albrecht, you're still the same old idiot as you always were," replied Wulf Martin disapprovingly. "Tell your guests they can sleep later. **There's a treat in store for them!**"

"Another story?"

"No. The polar lights."

---

for thrift's sake – aus Sparsamkeit; stride – Schritt;
There's a treat in store for them. – Da haben sie noch was Schönes zu erwarten.

The northern lights

Albrecht was suddenly wide awake and as if electrified. "Pull something on over your clothes, then get going! Try to get to the Uwe-Dune as quickly as possible! Or no, there are bound to be too many people there; they'll be in the way. Run up Strönwai and turn into Dünenweg. Go on, off you go!"

"Albrecht!"

"Go on!"

"Aren't you coming?"

"No, I've got my own little **vantage point**. Now get a move on, you **slow-coaches**!"

We **hared** down Sjipwai. Music and laughter were ringing out from the *Village Pitcher*; we ignored the lights on the main road, hurried through the people standing outside the pub, perfuming the air with expensive **scents** and celebrating the event with glasses in their hands. We reached Dünenweg, **dodged past** other light-watchers, and carried on until we had left everyone else behind us and had an uninterrupted view of the water and sky.

---

vantage point – günstiger Aussichtspunkt; slow-coach – Schlafmütze; to hare – wie ein geölter Blitz laufen; scent – Geruch; to dodge past – ausweichen

I stood in front of Carlos; he put his arms around me; and then we watched breathlessly as red **rays** of light flickered across the dark night sky; as green and yellow arrows **darted out** between them; as a transparent blue-grey **veil** spread itself out over the whole scene and vanished into nothingness; as a giant curved arch of yellow, red and pale turquoise stretched out across the night; as brilliant red streaks, yellow streaks and blue streaks drew **fiery patterns**; as they were obliterated and replaced by spinning arcs and golden spirals.

It seemed to us as if the air were **soaring** and buzzing. The rays and **shafts**, bows and arrows were above us, and yet it seemed as if we were standing right in the middle of them.

The speed with which the glowing apparitions were erased and created anew was breathtaking.

But the strangest, spookiest, most terrible thing about it was the absolute noiselessness of it all.

Now and then I looked down at the water. The sea was darker than the sky; only the **breakers** drew broad white **foam** arcs on the sand.

We couldn't say how long it lasted until the flickering and glowing above us became fainter and gradually came to an end. We stood and waited and almost hoped that an ear-splitting bang would **herald** the end of this firework display. But no bang came, and so we slowly emerged from our enchanted state and reluctantly made our way back.

---

ray – Strahl; to dart out – herausschießen; veil – Schleier; fiery – feurig; pattern – Muster; to soar – schwingen; shaft – Pfeil; breaker – Brecher; foam – Schaum; to herald – ankündigen

We didn't speak. Words would have been completely out of place.

But we did have a long kiss.

Only once we were outside Albrecht's little house did Carlos say, "I wonder if Albrecht has an encyclopaedia? I'd like to know how a polar light like that is created."

A light was burning in the front room. We thought Albrecht was waiting for us, but he had already gone to bed. However, as if he had anticipated Carlos' wish, an open book was lying on the little table next to his armchair. It was an encyclopaedia. "The northern lights, which flash across the sky at a height of 90 to 150 kilometres, only **occur** over the magnetic poles of the earth, where electrically **charged** particles of the sun are able to penetrate the earth's atmosphere. There they collide at high speed (200 km per second) with **nitrogen** and oxygen molecules which are thereby caused to glow."

"Reading is important," I said to Carlos. "But you know what? In this case, words are miles behind the experience, don't you reckon?"

"Absolutely. Hey, Mimi, are you tired?"

"I don't know. Why do you ask?"

"Do you remember Chile? The evening when we climbed up the dunes and watched the sunset?"

"Course I remember it! That was when everyone burst out with ooohs and aaahs, stretched their arms out to the sky, and acted as if they'd been **transported**!"

---

to occur – vorkommen; charged – geladen; nitrogen – Stickstoff; to be transported – hingerissen sein

"Precisely." Carlos grinned. "I'm so glad we were alone today."

I giggled. "Do you still remember how I then slid down the dunes and almost disappeared? Good job I was spared that one! We've already experienced a lot together, haven't we?"

Carlos nodded. "That welds people together. On Sylt, I sometimes feel really old."

"You what?"

"Well, after all, I am older than Holly and Constantin," he said, "but I wouldn't like to miss the island experiences."

"I can understand that. The geological-geomorphological faults are doubtless rather like a banquet for you. Anyway, have you any idea how late it is? Crikey, I need my beauty sleep; after all, I want to win first prize in the modelling competition!"

"Why? So you can start a new career? Model instead of travel writer?"

"Course not. So I can get a cheap trip to Berlin with you, Carlos!"

Jellyfish weather

When I woke up, jumped out of bed and banged my head on the roof beam as normal, I could feel that something had changed. I flung the window open: clear blue sky, bright sunshine, gentle wind. So it's not the weather that's changed, I thought, putting my bikini on with my jeans and shirt over the top.

But it *was* the weather.

"Easterly wind," said Märthe disapprovingly. "What a Schietkram! Easterly winds act like the Föhn in the Alps. People become quarrelsome, so watch out!"

"Will do!" I said, thinking of Johanna. Easterly wind or any wind at all, she was **in for it** today!

As Albrecht had predicted, Holly was already standing on the doormat before we'd drunk our first cup of coffee. She had sacrificed her beauty sleep for the northern lights experience and screwed up her nose when we said we wanted to go swimming first, competition or no competition.

"What are you going to wear? Did Constantin's mother **foist** a cashmere pullover on you?"

---

to be in for it – etwas zu erwarten haben;
to foist sth (up)on sb – jmdm. etwas aufdrängen

"Just wait and see!"

"Come on, show me!"

I was myself curious to see whether I liked the gear today as much as I had done the day before, so I ran up to my room and got changed. I had problems with the net stockings. The mesh was so far apart that I could only get them over my legs centimetre by centimetre. But they looked really fantastic with the red and white striped socks.

"Watch out!" I called from upstairs. "I'm coming!"

"Wow!" Holly's eyes almost popped out of her head.

Carlos was, however, not particularly enthusiastic.

"Don't you like it?"

"Of course, I like the outfit. I just think it's a bit too ... how can I put it ... a bit too sexy. Haven't you got anything else to wear?"

"Hey, I bought this especially! Now I'm **broke**!"

"What do *you* think, Holly?"

"Carlos, it's just ..." She held her hand in front of her mouth so that Märthe couldn't hear anything, and breathed, "... fabulous!"

I was satisfied. Where clothes were concerned, Holly's **verdict** counted for more than Carlos'.

When I had got changed again, we set off for the beach. The air was so mild and different from normal, the contours of the dunes so clear; and I was so happy that I cycled ahead of the other two all the way to the beach – on Albrecht's bike, as mine was, of course, still in Keitum.

---

to be broke – abgebrannt sein; verdict – Urteil

We immediately ran into Dirk and Kai.

"Stupid day today," Dirk said by way of greeting. "Jellyfish weather. We've already spotted **a couple**. Watch out if you're going in the water. If you see anything that looks like a **lump** of reddish blue gelatine, beat it at once, okay?"

"I know what jellyfish look like," said Carlos. "And I'll take care of Mimi."

"Good," said Dirk. "It would be a pity if you weren't fit and beautiful this evening, wouldn't it? Fit and beautiful – I don't get it!"

Johanna was coming! I stood in the sand with my legs apart and my **fists clenched**, waiting. I was ready for a fight. Bring it on.

"She's got a new bikini," stated Holly. "Seriously posh. Where did she get hold of that? I have to have a closer look at it."

Unfortunately, Johanna was being greeted by a young man with kisses to the left, right and left again. He put his arm round Johanna's waist and pulled her to the water. She evidently knew about the beauty-**enhancing** and revitalizing effect of the Sylt water.

The two of them plunged into the waves, squealing so loudly that it reached us. She had evidently not spotted us yet. Who knows, maybe she didn't want to see us either.

"Painful ... embarrassing," murmured Holly. "How can anyone make such a fuss!"

"How often do you get this jellyfish-bringing easterly wind?" Carlos wanted to know.

---

a couple – einige; lump – Klumpen; to clench one's fists – die Fäuste ballen; to enhance – steigern

"Can't say," replied Kai, shrugging his shoulders. "But when it's blowing, it can last for days."

"The wind isn't dangerous," explained Dirk. "The unpleasant thing about it is that the jellyfish appear by the west coast because they are driven along by the undercurrent, and this runs against the direction of the wind. It's difficult to explain that to people, but that's the way it is." He looked through his binoculars. "The white jellyfish aren't dangerous. The reddish blue and yellow ones are the nasty ones."

I only remembered bits of my biology lessons. "They're **stingers** with tentacles, and if you touch a tentacle, the effect's similar to a **nettle**, isn't it?"

"You really are just a clueless land-lubber, Mimi," Kai said kindly. "Listen: jellyfish are **predatory** stingers, that much is correct. In order to catch and eat their prey – plankton, little fish and crabs – they **anaesthetize** it. How do they do that? In every cell of their tentacles there's a rolled-up tube. When it's touched, the lid of the cell opens up, the tube whizzes out, and – bingo! – the prey is injected with a nasty **poisonous concoction**. What's the result? Little fish are eaten; big fish – and humans – scream 'Ouch!', feel rotten and look awful. What are the symptoms? Persistent, annoying **itching**; **rashes** and burning skin. Okay?"

"Well, that information was more comprehensive and better than anything I've ever heard before

---

stinger – Nesseltier; nettle – Brennnessel;
predatory – räuberisch; to anaesthetize – betäuben;
poisonous – giftig; concoction – Gebräu;
to itch – jucken; rash – Ausschlag

about these poison-makers. Oh yes, what does their poison consist of?"

"Don't act so innocent, Mimi. Who do you want to **bump off**?"

"Not you!" I laughed at him.

"Glad to hear it. Well, the poison consists of protein, foreign protein, which is particularly nasty, and **formic acid** – that's what hurts you when a little **ant** is trying to defend its life."

"But –"

"Kai!" cried Dirk. "Come over here!"

A mother was running across the sand carrying a **howling** child. "I bet that's the first jellyfish victim," said Dirk. "Kai, can you take care of the little one? You're better at it than I am."

Kai tried hard to adopt his most trust-inspiring expression and asked in a fatherly manner, "Hey, did that bad jellyfish stroke you? Where does it hurt?"

The child howled – not because of a jellyfish, but because she had cut her thumb on the edge of a mussel shell.

"It's bleeding!" sobbed the girl. "It hurts!"

"You know what? I'll say 'hocus pocus', hide the blood, and nothing will hurt any more. Shall I show you?"

The little girl nodded and a tear rolled down her cheek.

"Hocus pocus!" Kai stuck a plaster over the cut; the child gave one more sob; and then the pain vanished.

---

to bump off – um die Ecke bringen; formic acid – Ameisensäure; ant – Ameise; to howl – brüllen

"How's that? If something hurts again, you just come and see Kai the magician. He'll say hocus pocus and everything will be fine again. Promise?"

"Well, was I exaggerating? He knows what to do with children, doesn't he?" Dirk praised his friend with a slap on the back.

Holly, Carlos and I were just about to go into the water when Johanna and her companion ran towards us, yelling.

"I bet they've caught a jellyfish," said Kai.

And they had. Johanna was **clutching** her arm. "Do something!" she screamed. "Quickly! It's on fire!"

Dirk grabbed a yellow plastic bucket and poured water onto Johanna's arm. "That's the only thing that'll help," he explained. "Let me look now. Oh, he got you good and proper, Johanna."

"Today of all days!" she wailed. "The water's not done any good; haven't you got any **ointment**? Look, the marks are turning even redder!"

The places where the tentacles had touched Johanna's skin were, in fact, **beetroot** red and looked as if they had broken out in a rash.

Dirk scratched his head. "Looks as if they weren't all washed off."

He ran into the red hut and returned with a magnifying glass and a pair of tweezers. "Show me ... oh, it's not as bad as all that. You're not allergic to jellyfish **toxin**, are you?"

"How am I supposed to know?" Johanna retorted. "Will I be fit again this evening?"

---

to clutch – festhalten; ointment – Salbe;
beetroot – Rote Bete; toxin – Gift

"You'll be fit," Kai answered her question. "But the redness won't fade for a few days."

"Oh God. Whatever am I going to do?"

"Grin and bear it," Holly interrupted.

"Oh no," said Johanna furiously. "It's easy for you to talk: you're not taking part in the competition this evening."

Aha, so she really didn't know what was in store for her.

"Oh?" replied Holly. "We –"

I trod on her foot as a warning and cleared my throat. I'd have been better off not doing so.

"Just look at Mimi! The people on the campsite said that there was a girl in my tent. The description could fit you."

"Me in your *tent*?" I replied in astonishment. "Didn't you tell me you were staying at the *Stadt Hamburg* in Westerland? I've no idea whose tent our dog almost collapsed. In any case, we put it back up again. We didn't ask who it belonged to, did we, Carlos?"

"That's right. The whole business was so embarrassing!"

"On my last holiday, I crawled into the wrong tent one night. Thought it was mine, and it was **hilarious** how the owners reacted. Okay, so I disturbed them, but all the same. They nearly threw their shoes at my head," recounted Kai with a grin.

Johanna didn't fall for his **diversionary** tactic. "You knew that my tent was on the campsite and –"

"Maybe you moved?" Dirk interrupted her with

---

hilarious – lustig; diversionary – Ablenkungswide-eyed innocence. "We know lots of people who have to wait until a hotel room is available. That's always happening during the **peak season**, isn't it Kai?"

"You could say it's the order of the day on Sylt," Kai affirmed readily. "So where are you really staying, Johanna?"

"Nothing to do with you," she growled and pushed off with her companion.

"There was a great photo of you in the paper yesterday!" I called after her. "And a fantastic article about you! Does that mean you don't need me any more, Johanna?" She just made a **contemptuous** hand gesture and didn't even turn round.

"If you dig a grave for someone else, you end up falling into it yourself," Kai said with satisfaction. "You **defeated** her with her own arguments."

"Goodness only knows what she'll say when all six of us turn up at the modelling show this evening!" Holly rolled her eyes **with relish**. "It'll be brilliant!"

Two little boys had fished harmless white jellyfish out of the water and were throwing them at people like slippery gelatine balls. "That's going too far!" yelled Dirk. "Are you nuts? Jellyfish are living creatures, too!"

Carlos, Holly and I didn't fancy swimming any more. We agreed to meet at six o'clock at Westerland station. Holly promised to let Constantin know, and now Carlos and I had a long afternoon ahead of us.

---

peak season – Hochsaison; contemptuous – verächtlich; to defeat – besiegen; with relish – genießerisch

We stuffed our jeans and shirts into our bags and set off for a long walk along the beach. It was a fabulous day with occasional fat, white **puffy** clouds in the blue sky and a gentle easterly breeze. The sand beneath our feet was warm, and where the waves had dampened it, pleasantly firm. Once we had passed the famous 'Buhne 16', where all the stars and starlets of our parents' youth met and held glittering parties, the number of people with or without swimsuits constantly lessened.

Carlos and I always have something to talk about, but when the water speaks, the waves run onto the beach or crash back on themselves, it's better to keep out of it. We walked and walked; sometimes one of us bent down to pick up a mussel, pulled a piece of seaweed apart with our fingers, examined a **shard** of glass that had been smoothed and polished by the sand and the water, or silently pointed at a little lighthouse.

We approached the Klappholtal, a dune and nature reserve. "Do you want to go off the beach and into the dunes?" asked Carlos. "It's worth it. Holly said it was the biggest Wanderdünen area in Germany."

"Sounds incredibly like a gross exaggeration," I mocked. "Do you know if there happen to be *any* other Wanderdünen areas in the whole country?"

We laughed at one another, grasped one another's hands, and avoided a jellyfish that had been thrown up on the beach. A short distance from us, a person was **crouching**, his nose close to the ground. "He's looking for something," said Carlos.

---

puffy – bauschig; shard – Scherbe; to crouch – kauern

"Mussels," I said **laconically**.

To our surprise, we discovered as we came closer that it was Wulf Martin. "Are you looking for something?" I burst out.

Groaning, he stood up. "It's an easterly wind today," he said, "and that's when I always go to the beach to look for **amber**. Look what I've found."

In the palm of his hand there lay a couple of tiny transparent brownish and orangey **crumbs**. "I've not made any big discoveries today," he said. "But if it hasn't happened yet, it can still happen."

"I thought you only found amber at **the Baltic**," I said, baffled.

Wulf Martin shook his head. "Lots of people think that. But it's not the case. Do you know anything about amber?"

He had found the right partner in Carlos, who **let rip**, "Of course, we know about it. Amber is **petrified resin** that's millions of years old. It comes from pine-trees that once used to cover large areas of Scandinavia, and reacted by giving off resin if ever they were damaged. The resin had an intensive aroma and attracted insects and also larger animals that got stuck there. They were enclosed in the resin and died. The sea invaded at some point, locking the resin into an **airtight** lump, with the result that it solidified and stayed that way." Carlos paused. "Anything else?"

"Why not?" replied Wulf Martin. "You've not told me anything new yet!"

---

laconic – wortkarg; amber – Bernstein, crumb – Krümel;
the Baltic – Ostsee; to let rip – loslegen;
petrified – erstarrt; resin – Harz; airtight – luftdicht

Carlos grinned. "I'm sure you know more about it than I do. The ice age **glaciers** pushed the resin southwards, the melt-water floated it into the Baltic and North Sea – and to the Sylt coast as well. People also call amber the 'gold of the north'."

"Funny, the way that things are always compared to gold," I said. "Salt is 'white gold', amber is 'northern gold'."

"Gold was the most valuable thing that humans could imagine," explained Wulf Martin. "What always surprises me is that even the people in the oldest known graves wore amber amulets. Do you know Denghoog? No? It's a 5,000-year-old cave near the little pond in Wenningstedt, with a six-metre-long path leading into it. Even there, they found individual amber pearls along with bits of human **skeletons**."

Wulf Martin pushed the tiny pieces around the palm of his hand with his cracked **thumbnail**. "The traders took the 'gold of the north' from our coasts to the Adriatic and to the south of France."

He picked up a bright little **speck** on the end of his finger. "White amber was regarded as a medicine for all illnesses." He laughed suddenly. "It was probably the insane prices that drove all the ill people straight out of their beds!" He examined us with his sharp eyes. "I've no doubt you also know, Carlos, that amber was very important for us seafarers."

Carlos frowned. "So far as I know, people turned the raw material into an extremely resistant **varnish** which was used to paint boats."

---

glacier – Gletscher; skeleton – Skelett; thumbnail – Daumennagel; speck – Fleck; varnish – Lack, Glasur

Wulf Martin's eyebrows shot up. "Heavens above! Not many land-lubbers know that!"

Carlos and Wulf Martin chatted for a short while longer about how the varnish had been made, and I cursed myself for not having my notebook with me. "Doesn't matter," Carlos consoled me. "I'll help you write it up when we get home." Home! We looked at the time and realized that we had to get a serious move on. We said goodbye to Wulf Martin and ran down the beach towards Kampen.

"Do you know what I like best about Sylt?" I panted. "If you're away from the main beach, you think you're on an isolated island. A couple of minutes later you're in a completely different world. You run into the most chic boutiques you could possibly imagine. It's fantastic, isn't it?"

"You've forgotten the custom-built car, Mimi!" Carlos pointed to a dark green Jaguar. "I wouldn't mind driving that one day!"

The end of airs and graces!

Pandemonium broke out in Albrecht's little house. After Carlos had showered, I took over the bathroom. I washed my hair three times and my bikini once. I left my hair to dry naturally and dried my bikini with the hairdryer, then I stuffed it together with my – ironed! – jeans, T-shirt and the brand-new clothes into my rucksack, packed my little make-up bag on top of them and pulled the cord shut. I sacrificed my notebook. It was too dangerous to take it with me.

I ran down the stairs and straight into Albrecht.

"Have you seen today's paper?" he wanted to know. "No? You should have a quick look at this article!"

That was the last thing I wanted to do. I did it all the same, though. "Stories from History: Part Two," I read. JE had written something about a seaman who had sailed the East Indian waters and had brought back with him a saying: the dragon only rises up against the wind!

"Märthe told me that!" I cried furiously. "That really is the limit!"

---

airs and graces – Starallüren

"Keep your eyes open: JE is bound to be in the hall," said Albrecht. "Off you go, now, I'll drive you. But Märthe and Wulf Martin and I will be there by ten o'clock."

I'd been cool and relaxed all day, but now my hands were **clammy** and my heart was pounding. Constantin and Holly were standing at Westerland station, and squashed into the car with us. My heartbeat increased to become a violent drumming, and when we got out at the airport, my legs had turned to jelly.

Holly said she felt just the same as me. **Beads** of sweat were standing out on Constantin's upper lip, and Carlos suddenly started cursing, "What a complete load of nonsense! I'm withdrawing my application!"

"You can't chicken out at the last moment," croaked Holly. "Do you think I feel any better?"

"How do you know how I feel?" **countered** Carlos.

Constantin hung his head and trotted silently alongside us. All sorts of people in the most fantastic party clothes were standing around and blocking the way. We **squeezed** through with difficulty and found ourselves standing in the hall.

My God, it was enormous! There were two levels, countless **fake** palm trees, a middle area which had been repackaged as a bar – and the catwalk.

A red catwalk.

I suddenly felt paralysed. I'm supposed to walk

---

clammy – klamm; bead – Perle; to counter – entgegnen; to squeeze – (sich) quetschen; fake – falsch across this thing? I asked myself. Past all these loads of people? Mimi, courage is just a matter of training: you've said A, so all you need to say is B. Go on then ...

Carlos had grabbed my arm and was pulling me along. "Where will we find the people who know what's what?"

"No idea ... There are Kai and Dirk! Hello!"

The pair grinned with some effort. "Do you really think we should?" asked Kai. "I mean, I'm not so sure now. It looks to me like a real test of courage, don't you reckon?"

The only one who suddenly didn't have any **inhibitions** was Holly. Priska found us. "Glad you're taking part!" she yelled above the other people's heads. "Most people have got cold feet and they've withdrawn their applications. Come with me!"

She guided us through the crowd. The hall had been divided somewhere by **partition walls** behind which were the "dressing rooms": one for the boys and the other for us.

"So, this is how it works," explained Priska. "You wear jeans and a T-shirt for the pre-casting. Whoever doesn't look good is eliminated. This is followed by the walk in individual leisurewear and ..."

"... whoever turns up looking uncool is out," murmured Kai. "Oh God, this will do nothing for my **self-esteem**, honestly!"

Priska ignored him. "Finally, you appear in swimming trunks or a bikini. Okay?"

"How do we know when it's our turn?" asked

---

inhibition – Hemmung; partition wall – Trennwand; self-esteem – Selbstachtung

Holly. She had strong nerves! I'd have liked to run away, and she was asking what order we were to go in!

"No problem. Before it happens, you'll get a number. Everything okay?" She looked at the piece of paper that she was holding in her hand. "Who's Dirk?"

"I am."

"Kai? Holly? Mimi? Carlos? Constantin?"

Constantin was missing. In all the **commotion** we only noticed it now.

"I don't believe it!" moaned Holly. "He has actually got cold feet. Well, I think that's rotten, honestly I do."

"I don't," contradicted Kai. "I still don't know whether I'm going to drop out."

Priska shoved the boys energetically towards the dressing rooms. "No way! We need every applicant we can get!"

"So how many boys are there?" asked Holly.

"These three and one more. He's called Klaus. You know, the one who's my boyfriend. But he hasn't turned up yet." Priska shook her head. "Boys are always so **unreliable**. When they see the catwalk at the latest, all that's left of their courage-buffet is crumbs. It's a lousy performance."

"Mimi!" Carlos was standing behind me, waving me to one side. "I'm not doing it. I'll wash dishes or labour on a **building site** or something so that we can afford our Berlin trip. But that there –" he pointed with his chin to the **seething** masses, "that

---

commotion – Tumult; unreliable – unzuverlässig; building site – Baustelle; to seethe – wimmeln

there is too much for me. It'll leave you free to do whatever you like, okay?"

"What do you mean by that?" I asked, dumbfounded.

"Nnnnnothing, well, nothing special. I just want to say that I'll keep my fingers crossed for you, okay?"

Kai was suddenly standing next to him. "Mate, I'll cross my fingers for the girls, too. It's much more **commendable** than trudging down that **weird** carpet there."

"Okay. See you!" Hey presto! Carlos and Kai had gone. Simply gone.

"You're staying!" Priska pushed open the dressing room door and gave Dirk an energetic shove inside.

I started to sweat. Of course, I knew that the hall was big and that huge numbers of people would come. But I hadn't reckoned on such masses even in my dreams.

"Hey, when the music's banging, they'll all be partying. Barely anyone will be looking at you," Priska assured me. "Don't *you* lot **leave me in the lurch** as well, okay?"

"If you chicken out, I'm chickening out, too," said Holly.

"Are you chickening out, Mimi?" asked Priska.

I raised my shoulders, undecided. "I don't know ... What are we doing this all for? I definitely don't want to be a model. I'm just taking part to win the trip to Berlin."

---

commendable – empfehlenswert; weird – unheimlich; to leave sb in the lurch – jmdn. im Stich lassen

"And to teach Johanna a lesson," Holly reminded me. "Don't you think that's worth it? But I'll tell you, I'm asking myself why we're putting ourselves through all this."

"Johanna?" asked Priska. "Is that the tall blonde one? She's already here."

Holly drew up her shoulders. "Well then, let's do it!"

Boldly she pushed open the door. A cloud of perfume hit us. Hairspray hung in the air, and in a mirror I spotted a pale girl leaning against the wall, her eyes wide with horror. It was me!

"What have *you two* lost here?" Johanna's left eye was prominently displayed in a silver frame; the right one was still blank.

Up until this question I had been on the verge of chickening out like Carlos and helping him wash dishes. But when someone asks me what I've "lost" in a particular place, it makes me cross. Then my **hackles** rise, and **woe betide** anyone who gets near me. Especially, when I don't just **have a bone to pick with** the person, but a whole **carcass**.

"The question is justified, Johanna," I replied as coolly as possible, folding my arms across my chest. I scrutinized her from top to bottom, then turned casually to Holly, screwing up my nose. "What has Johanna lost here? We heard she'd withdrawn her application, didn't we?"

"Me? Withdrawn my application? Why should I do a thing like that?!" she snapped.

---

hackles – Nackenhaare; woe betide – wehe; to have a bone to pick with sb – mit jmdm. ein Hühnchen zu rupfen haben; carcass – Kadaver; to snap – schimpfen

"The reasons that were put to us are so awful that we wouldn't like to repeat them," I replied.

"That's right." Holly took a little shirt from Johanna's chair and held it up. "I wonder whether she bought that or ... you know, Mimi."

"You mean whether she **lawfully acquired** it or whether ... incredibly enough, and at the appropriate time, somebody 'lost' it?"

"That's exactly what I mean," sighed Holly. "You wouldn't believe how unscrupulous some people are."

Johanna turned bright red. The colour didn't suit her. I told her that, and Holly agreed completely.

Unfortunately, Priska shoved three further candidates into the dressing room at that moment. Instead of feeling like startled rabbits, they scrutinized us without any embarrassment. It was immediately obvious to Holly and me: the three of them were experienced.

They marched past us and up to Johanna.

"Hey! I'm Sylvia," the first one introduced herself.

Sylvia was mega-thin, as tall as Johanna, and she had the most perfect **page-boy haircut** I'd ever seen. She looked enviable. French. Sexy. Elegant.

"Are you using that powder? I'd never do that. Everyone knows that powder blocks your pores and can trigger allergies. What's that there? An allergy?" Sylvia inspected critically the red marks on Johanna's upper arm.

"I bumped into a jellyfish when I was swimming," she explained.

---

lawful – gesetzmäßig; to acquire – erwerben;
page-boy haircut – Pagenschnitt

"Oh? Today? I see. Well, I'd say that, too, if I were you. Who's going to admit to having an allergy if they want to cut a good figure at a casting?"

"It's not an allergy, it really is –"

"You don't have to pretend with me," Sylvia interrupted her. "It's just between us, isn't it? But I think I'd prefer to move my chair a little bit away from yours. Better safe than sorry. Hey, Vera, come on! I'm sure Johanna will be so kind as to move down to the end of the row of mirrors. You'll do that, won't you?"

"Crikey, Johanna, that rash looks truly revolting. Are you sure it's not **contagious**? I mean, it's uncool to put other people at risk, I really don't think that's funny. That really is the end of airs and graces!"

"You have no idea how right you are, Sylvia!" said Holly, and then we both burst out laughing.

---

contagious – ansteckend

Painting lesson

Vera had short black hair, a pale **complexion**, and was wearing blood-red lipstick. Not my type, but someone who was into that kind of thing would doubtless find her **stunning**.

The third one of the trio was Victoria. Victoria wasn't beautiful. She was, it's true, very tall and very thin, but she had a large **bust**, and her nose was too long and slightly crooked, and her eyes weren't exactly what the advertising people call "big and bright". Her hair was the best thing about her: long and **curly**. Not frizzy, not tangled, no; it tumbled down to her shoulders in fine waves and large curls. I sighed. Victoria had exactly the hair I'd always wanted.

The three got stuck into their make-up and Holly and I squeezed into the row. I was ready first: mascara, lipstick, gloss on top. Done.

Fascinated, I watched what the others were doing to themselves. "Well, hello, Johanna!" cried Sylvia, horrified. "You're not squeezing your **spots** now are you? Are you nuts?"

---

complexion – (Gesichts-)Farbe; stunning – toll; bust – Busen; curly – lockig; spot – Pickel

"Nnnno, I've just –"

"Leave her alone," Vera interrupted. "One competitor fewer gives us a better chance. Hey, little one, is that it?"

I started. "Do you mean me?"

"Who else? You do look really sweet with your frizzy hair, but you presumably don't intend to put any colour on your face?"

"I thought it was fine," I defended myself.

"Girl, the first spotlights will make you look like a corpse. Wait until I've finished. I'll help you, okay?"

"If you think so?!"

"Of course I think so," she said decisively.

Half an hour later she turned to me. "So, let me have a go."

She had stuck on individual false **eyelashes** and had made her face up so that it looked completely different – but great, simply great.

She slapped some "pre-make-up" onto my face, rubbed it around with a little sponge and told me, "Never use plastic, okay? Only ever use a natural sponge."

"Hmmm."

Then she applied the actual make-up and tapped around on my face like mad. "Do you know the tapping technique? You spread the colour around by gently tapping with your fingertips."

"Hmmm."

"Hey, Sylvia, do you think this tone is suitable for Mimi? She's quite brown, so maybe I should choose a darker colour."

---

eyelashes – Wimpern

Sylvia put her head on one side. "I wouldn't. A **trace** of **blusher** on her cheeks and under her eyebrows, and it'll be perfect."

"You're right." Vera worked concentratedly. "How come you're so good at this?" I asked.

"Shh, don't talk! I want to be a make-up artist and I only applied so that I could get experience on set."

"Really?"

"Yes."

I shut my mouth like a good girl.

She brushed on blue-green eye-shadow and shaded my eyebrows in brown. She applied more lip-liner and added a brownish red with a brush – I'd never have chosen the colour of my own accord, but it went well. Finally, she sprayed water over her work of art and held a mirror up to my face. "Well, what do you reckon?"

I was **gobsmacked** and cried, "What? Is that me?"

"Absolutely top class!" **affirmed** Holly enviously.

"Now it's your turn," said Vera brightly, combing Holly's hair down her back. "Have you got any hoop earrings? Big ones?"

"No," said Holly regretfully.

"Doesn't matter. I've got some with me." Vera had a make-up bag the size of my aunt Lise's shopping bag. She rummaged around in it for a good while, then clipped two hoops the size of footballs onto Holly's ears. "That's just as I'd imagined it," she murmured, twisting Holly's hair into a thick left-sided plait.

---

trace – Spur; blusher – Rouge; gobsmacked – baff, platt; to affirm – bestätigen

"Holly! You look like a spirited **gypsy**," I said in astonishment.

"Just look what a difference proper styling makes."

Vera looked around and screwed up her nose. "So, Johanna, are you happy with how you look?"

"Of course."

Admittedly, Johanna looked very good. Her hair was shining, and now she was using a thick brush to apply glittery powder to her décolleté. Vera, however, shook her head and turned away in disgust. "That looks like artificial snow powder on a Christmas decoration," she murmured **disparagingly**. "The woman needs colour."

"Oh?" Johanna applied lipstick of the palest pink. "Well, I don't agree."

"We'll see who's right," replied Vera calmly.

"Isn't there anything to drink here?" asked Sylvia. "I'll fetch us something."

"Diet cola for me." I almost jumped out of my skin: these were Victoria's first words.

And then I did in fact miss a breath. Victoria wasn't Victoria any more: she was *the* greatest beauty of all.

With a critical expression she squeezed mousse onto the palm of her hand and rubbed it into her hair. She repeated this at least ten times, but then her curls and waves had three times their normal volume. "Don't they all collapse?" I asked.

She shook her head. "Not if you use a lot of mousse."

Here I was, learning yet more life-skills!

---

gypsy – Zigeunerin; disparaging – geringschätzig

The music had long since been booming and humming in the hall. We were starting to become restless, but it wasn't until a good hour later that Priska came in. "It's starting in a minute. Are you ready?"

She didn't look at our appearance, but simply pressed pieces of cardboard numbered from one to six into our hands. Not only that, but they were also in alphabetical order! "So that it's all fair," she explained.

"Hey, Priska, how many boys are ready?" Sylvia wanted to know.

"Two."

"Two boys and six girls – and all this fuss!" **marvelled** Holly.

"Rubbish." Victoria crossed her long legs. "We're just a little addition to the big party!"

And that was indeed the case. When it was finally our turn, the hall was going wild, but only the people standing along the edge of the red carpet even noticed us. All the others were far too preoccupied with themselves.

On the one hand, I was quite glad; on the other, I felt cross about the money I'd spent on new clothes. And I could fully understand Carlos. The whole effort was, of course, a waste of time.

The jury, which consisted of Priska, two other women and three men, decided that as there were so few participants, there was no need to bother with the pre-casting. So we six girls and Dirk, together with Priska's boyfriend Klaus, only walked down the carpet twice.

---

to marvel – staunen

Dirk stumbled once. Klaus **gave** the last round – the swimming costume one – **a miss**, on the grounds that he had a **pigeon chest** and a bottom which was, unfortunately, not perfectly tight.

Only on my second walk down the carpet did I spot my Carlos. He, Constantin and Kai had organized balloons and little flags and were waving them like mad, yelling "Mi-mi, Mi-mi!" and "Hol-ly, Hol-ly!" at the tops of their voices. That completely **put me off my stride**. I stopped to wave and blow kisses at them. Holly twigged too late; **jostled** straight **into** me, thereby ruining the net stockings which had turned ordinary clothes into a **top-notch** outfit – **albeit** one that I'd probably never have worn at home.

Vera had been right: Johanna looked **insipid** and **nondescript** in her white jeans and little white shirt. The strong spotlights did in fact swallow up all her colour. "What did I say? Anyone with no charisma has to wear colour. And in any case, shimmery powder only works close up."

Incidentally, the audience was so excited by us that they turned us all into winners by cheering and clapping, and after detailed discussions, the jury made their decisions: winner and first runner-up among the boys were Dirk and Klaus.

With us girls (there were, of course, not just two of us!) the order was like this: first place: Victoria;

---

to give a miss – auslassen; pigeon chest – Hühnerbrust; to put sb off one's stride – jmdn. aus dem Konzept bringen; to jostle into – anrempeln; top-notch – fantastisch; albeit – obgleich; insipid – fade; nondescript – unauffällig; incidental – zufällig

first runner-up: Sylvia; Vera, Holly, Johanna and I were all second runners-up.

We proudly accepted our certificates and showed them to the audience, the majority of whom were, unfortunately, busy dancing, flirting and **canoodling**, and refrained from giving us a standing ovation. So what, I could understand that.

Carlos was waiting for me with a packet of wet-wipes and wiped most of the paint off my face before he gave me a victory kiss and handed me over to Märthe, Albrecht and Wulf Martin.

Suddenly, Constantin was standing by us. "Coward! Disappearing without a word!" I grumbled, but still let him take me in his arms and kiss me.

We all slapped one another on the back and were just glad that all this nonsense was over.

Nobody could talk amidst the heaving crowd, **on account of which** Albrecht immediately wanted to take himself off elsewhere. "Are you staying, or are you coming with me?"

"Out of the question! After all that work we want to have an evening at last!" Holly cried spiritedly.

Albrecht went off with Märthe and Wulf Martin. Märthe, however, came back one last time. "Mimi, the tall insipid blonde, who looked a bit naffed off on the catwalk, is standing over there with the guy from the newspaper."

"Where?" I **craned my neck** and stood on tiptoe. "Thanks, Märthe!"

I wound my way through to them. "Hello, Jens-Uwe, we've been looking for you."

---

to canoodle – knutschen, schmusen; on account of which – weswegen; to crane one's neck – den Hals recken

"Wh-why?" He wasn't entirely **sober**, that guy. "D'you wanna be in the papers, too? You're too late. Hey, where'll I find this Victoria, eh?"

"Don't worry, I shan't keep you. But I've read your articles. Blimey, you can't half write! If only I were as good as you!"

"Yeah, can't I just?" He beamed.

"There is, of course, also the question of how you get the right information," I continued. "Could you tell me your sources?"

"Course I could ..."

"Come on, Jens-Uwe, that's got nothing to do with Mimi," Johanna interrupted, trying to drag him away.

"Wh-why's th-at?" He **disentangled** himself. "Look, Mimi, in our profession there's no such thing as a free lunch, geddit? You **scratch** my back, I'll scratch yours. I did an interview with Johanna, and she squeezed stuff out of everyone she knows in return. Collected sht-sht-shtories, okay?"

"Which she wrote down for you?"

"Nah, not wrote down; I take care of the writing part. She told me the sht-sht-shtories."

"Clever!"

"Said so ... you scratch my back, I'll scratch yours."

"Fantastic!"

"Fantastic," he affirmed. "C'n you take me to Vich-victoria now?"

"I've got no idea where she is ... I'll just ask the others, okay?"

---

sober – nüchtern; to disentangle yourself – sich losmachen; to scratch – kratzen

It really was pure coincidence that I bumped into Victoria outside the loos. And it was also pure coincidence, honestly, that it occurred to me to say just as I saw her, "Hey, Victoria, could you spare me five minutes?"

"Why?"

I told her in a couple of sentences why I was on the island.

"I'm writing about the competition and I'd like to ask you, as the winner, a couple of questions. I would, of course, send you the article. Do you fancy it?"

She looked me up and down and laughed. "Have you got paper and a pencil?"

I had them no more than I had my notebook, but we got hold of a menu and she lent me her lip-pencil.

I wrote: *Victoria is the* ***radiant*** *winner. She's characterized by perfect skin, sparkling eyes, a wonderful mane of hair and, of course, a perfect figure.*

"I know who I am, what I like, and how I want to look," she explained. "I enjoy success; I enjoy the fact that I could experience this evening; I enjoy the fact that I was lucky."

"But you partly create your own luck."

"Oh yes! My greatest achievement is working hard for my success."

"How do you do that?"

"I stay true to myself; I have my own opinions and I don't let myself be ***put off by failure****."*

---

radiant – strahlend; to be put off by failure – sich von einem Misserfolg entmutigen lassen

Victoria was by no means finished. Unfortunately, her soft lip-pencil had worn out, and there was no more space for a further statement on the menu.

"What a pity! Thanks very much, Victoria! By the way, the reporter from the Sylt local paper is looking for you. It wouldn't do your image any harm if he were to feature you tomorrow."

"Thanks for the tip!" Victoria checked her hair. "Could you give me my lip-liner back? And don't forget to send me the article."

"No worries!" I cried and ran off to the others.

"Where were you? I was starting to worry about you," said Carlos in my ear.

"Oh, Carlos, if only you knew what I'd experienced in the last few minutes!"

"Was it more Schietkram?"

"Course not!" I told him about Victoria and that Märthe had pointed out Jens-Uwe to me. "You didn't notice in all the **hustle and bustle**. I now know for sure that Johanna stole my notebook – and above all, why." I **filled him in on** the **deal** that the pair had struck.

Carlos stared at me. "Now I understand everything. I don't believe it! After she'd finally realized that you didn't write for the Sylt paper, she had to act quickly so that her interview would still be published in time. And Jens-Uwe let himself be drawn into it! You know what, Mimi? It's too hot in here for me; too stuffy and **stale** and constricted. Do you want to stay longer?"

---

hustle and bustle – reges Treiben; to fill sb in on sth – jmdn. über etwas informieren; deal – Abmachung; stale – verbraucht (Luft)

Disco lights flashed over our heads and I suddenly remembered the northern lights.

"No," I said firmly. "I want to leave. I've had enough."

I saw Holly and pushed my way through the crowd to her. "Carlos and I are pushing off, okay?"

"But it's only just starting, Mimi!"

"Yes, but –"

"Constantin!" yelled Holly. "Wait!" With one bound she was at his side and pulled him onto the dance-floor without further ado.

From what I knew of Holly, she'd make sure she had a great evening with Constantin!

Unimaginably great!

I slept long into the morning and only woke up when someone ran a wet cloth across my face and simultaneously directed a hot, foul-smelling hair-dryer at me. "Noballs! Leave me alone!"

Noballs barked, dragged the covers onto the floor and landed on my bed. I laughed and cursed, got up and bumped into Carlos in the bathroom. He looked just as unslept and peepy-eyed as I did.

Albrecht, by contrast, was most cheerful. He had made coffee that was at least three times stronger than Märthe's, who wouldn't arrive until later in the day. I would, in fact, have liked to tell him about Johanna's and Jens-Uwe's deal, but that was impossible. He kept walking to and fro, asking questions like, "Do the **freesias** go in this green vase? What do you think? Is the white one even nicer? … Does the room seem formal or cosy to you? … White sugar with tea isn't true to style, but lots of people don't like brown. The best thing is to offer all kinds, isn't it? Brown sugar lumps, white sugar lumps and all sorts of rock candy. Or do you think that's a bit exaggerated?"

---

freesia – Freesie

"Don't **strain yourself**, Albrecht," murmured Carlos. "We're modest folk."

"Who's talking about you? I'm thinking of the guests who are coming this afternoon."

Heavens above, Carlos and I hadn't given them another thought. And that was why he was making all this fuss? "They're just a load of old acquaintances," I said with a yawn.

"Not just, not just!" Albrecht polished a candlestick and tested to see if a white or pale green candle looked better in it.

I asked cautiously, "Are you all right, or did the coffee not agree with you?"

From the **moth-proof** chest that calls itself the brain, he had dug up an ancient song by the Beatles and was in fact humming 'Yesterday ...'.

Evidently, something wasn't as normal. I found it unpleasant and nudged Carlos. "Shall we go for a swim?" We had the impression that Albrecht was glad to be able to realize his **beautification frenzy** undisturbed. We were further unsettled by the fact that he impressed upon us at least ten times that we had to be back punctually at three o'clock.

We tramped through the sand and lay down in the sun next to Kai and Dirk. Neither of them was as 'up' as normal either, and they were both glad that there was no fierce westerly wind throwing up waves nor a rustling easterly wind to make jellyfish **accumulate** in the water.

---

to strain oneself – sich anstrengen; moth-proof – mottensicher; beautification frenzy – Verschönerungswahn; to accumulate – anhäufen

"Are you up already?" Dirk asked disbelievingly. "If I were you, I'd have slept until midday."

"Was it that late?" asked Carlos.

"We were in our **bunks** just before six."

"Bunks?"

"Yes. We just put our heads down here in the hut. There was no point using the bed for the sake of two hours. By the way, Johanna caused more trouble."

"Tell all!"

Dirk grinned broadly; you couldn't get a broader grin. "Victoria and I were celebrating our win. Well, anyone in our position would have done, wouldn't they? Jens-Uwe from the Sylt paper was by that late stage pretty hyper. He took a whole load of photos of us and dragged us off into a quieter corner where he tried to press us for information: what we were up to, how we felt now, what our hobbies were, our goals, whether we were going to Berlin together – he wanted to know all that rubbish.

All of a sudden, Johanna appeared and started cursing him.

'You promised to do an interview with me!'

'Are you the winner or is Victoria?' asked Jens-Uwe.

'I'm the second runner-up, at any rate!' cried Johanna. 'We had a deal! I kept my side of it; I gave you the material!'

'The deal only applied if you won first prize!'

No idea what it meant. Whatever, she started to hit Jens-Uwe and completely lost it."

"We know why," I said and told him about the deal Johanna had made with Jens-Uwe.

---

bunk – Koje

Dirk and Kai were flabbergasted. "So that's why she stole your notebook and told him your stories from it. And in return he was supposed to feature her in the paper, firstly as favourite then as winner of the modelling competition. I have to say, she worked that one nicely!"

"Only the plan didn't work out, unfortunately," smirked Dirk. The pair of them were so delighted by Johanna's failure that they immediately organized a game of volleyball!

Shortly after three o'clock we were standing outside Albrecht's white garden gate.

"My God, where have you been?" he shouted.

"It is all happening? Do you need cakes? Sugar candy? Milk? What's missing?"

"The guests will be here any minute!"

Märthe just shook her head. Of course, she had laid the table with loving care and had prepared three types of cake and a plate of biscuits – but she had no idea why Albrecht was so **het up** either. "I've never known him be like this," she whispered to us as he moved the chairs a couple of millimetres around the table for the millionth time. "If I didn't know how old he was, I'd say he was in love. But at *that* age?! Oh well, we'll soon be the wiser. Prick up your ears and **keep your eyes peeled**!"

The first guest was Wulf Martin. Of course, he lived nearby. Holly and Tom Thoms were next. Tom Thoms immediately pulled his pipe out of his trouser pocket and began to fill it. "Out of the ques-

---

to be het up – aufgeregt/erregt sein;
to keep one's eyes peeled – die Augen offen halten

tion," cried Albrecht in horror. "Tobacco smoke pollutes the whole house!"

Astonished, Tom Thoms put his pipe back in his pocket. "You're a bit naffed off, aren't you? It's the first time you've ever had anything against my pipe."

"What? What did you say? No, I've not got anything at all against your pipe, Tom, how could I?"

Albrecht scurried backwards and forwards between the door and the table.

"Well, I should hope not." Satisfied, Tom Thoms filled his pipe.

"Didn't I tell you not to pollute the house with your smoke?" Albrecht wrenched the window open and wafted the smoke out into the open air with a **napkin**.

We were gradually starting to doubt whether he was still all there. The doorbell rang for a third time.

"Märthe, close the window! Märthe, open the door, no, let me do it. Märthe take this napkin from me, Märthe, get on with it!!!"

"Oh God, the man's gone senile," said Wulf Martin concernedly.

Tom Thoms finally lit his pipe.

"He's always been a bit of a **nutter**," said Märthe.

"Constantin, what lovely fabric your trousers are made of!" cried Holly and flung her arms around him.

Suddenly there was a deadly silence.

"Susanne."

"Albrecht."

I thought I'd suddenly landed in a film: Susanne and Albrecht were standing at the door, staring at one another, staring and staring – without a word.

---

napkin – Serviette; nutter – Spinner/-in

It was kitschy and slushy and so moving that my eyes were wet, and I simply had to put my arms around Carlos.

Finally, Susanne brushed her hair from her forehead with that characteristic elegant movement. Noballs was the first to find his voice again; he howled **heart-rendingly** and threw himself at Albrecht's feet. Albrecht patted him and just said, "Everything's fine!"

Albrecht led Susanne into the room, introduced her, set her chair in place, disappeared – and returned with a gigantic bunch of long-stemmed roses. White, not red roses.

"I got them in case you really were *the* Susanne whom I've never forgotten all these years," he said in a husky voice. "Twenty of them. As before."

"Only they're white today," whispered Susanne.

Carlos and I held hands; Tom's pipe didn't want to draw; Märthe smiled, moved; Wulf Martin scraped his feet uncomfortably; and Constantin looked at his hands, embarrassed.

Holly was the only one you could rely on, "Don't say you know one another!" she cried. "Albrecht, are you the man who took Susanne out on her 20th birthday? She told us the story!"

He nodded, but he didn't **divulge** any further details now and in the present company.

We drank tea – with milk and sugar! – and ate cakes, but there was no real atmosphere. The questions: "What happened then? Why did Albrecht never forget Susanne? Is she the reason he never

---

heart-rending – herzzerreißend;
to divulge – bekanntgeben

married? What will happen between them now?" stood in the room as if written in capital letters.

Only once, when Wulf Martin gave me two little lumps of amber and told me when and where he had found them, did the conversation become more animated. Pretty soon, Wulf Martin and Tom Thoms left, but Holly had no intention of accompanying her grandfather, yet on the other hand, it was clear to us all that Susanne and Albrecht wanted to be alone.

So Holly and Constantin, Carlos and I wandered through Kampen and climbed up onto the Uwe-Dune platform for one last time. We leant against the railings and looked out across the sea.

We'd experienced so much this week: Carlos had pulled the little girl out of the water; the fog in the tidal flats had taken away my sight; and Johanna had made for all sorts of excitements. With the stories from Sylt's past and a brand-new story about the modelling competition, I had enough material for my teen pages. But the real adventure was the one Carlos and I had been through. We now knew that we had to be on our guard for human troublemakers, but we also knew that we could rely on one another. I looked over at Holly. She was standing quite close to Constantin, whispering something in his ear; he put his arm around her shoulders and then – no, they weren't kissing. But it looked pretty much as if the two would be linked by more than a holiday acquaintanceship.

The pair had evidently felt my gaze on them. "These have been exciting days," said Constantin. "A week ago I didn't know how I was going to get rid of Johanna. But now I'm glad that she stuck to me like chewing-gum – I'd never have got to know you all if it weren't for her."

"True," said Holly. "Without her, you'd only ever had had your nose stuck in books, and we'd never have taken part in the modelling competition. That was fun! Just a pity that you guys chickened out at the last minute!"

"It's enough that you saw it through!" said Carlos, pulling me to him. "I was full of admiration for you, but anyone who knows Mimi knows that it won't be her last mad act. It'll be interesting to see what happens to us!"

Constantin brushed his hair off his forehead. "You'll stay together. And Holly and I ..."

"Yes?" asked Holly in anticipation. "What about us?"

"Do you know?" replied Constantin shyly.

"Well, of course!" **Impetuously**, Holly flung her arms around his neck.

"I wish you heaps of luck," said Carlos. "Hopefully, you'll have an easier time with Holly than I have with Mimi. Being with her isn't half exhausting, Constantin! If you knew all I went through in Chile and Morocco – not to mention the Abruzzi. But I wouldn't split up with her for anything in the world."

"Constantin! What do you say to that?" cried Holly. Then – at last! they kissed. Of course, we followed their example!

The next morning everyone accompanied us to the station and gave us their farewell presents.

---

impetuous – ungestüm

Märthe gave us home-made Frisian biscuits; Constantin gave us a copy of *Der Schimmelreiter* together with a dried **starfish**; Susanne had bought me a new pair of net stockings; Holly gave Carlos a little stone, telling him earnestly that it was a little piece of a geological-geomorphological fault; Dirk had filled a bag with mussels and Kai a jam jar with Sylt sand. And Albrecht? "I promised you a present at the start of the week, Carlos. Do you remember?"

"That's right!" I cried. "I got the notebook, and you said you'd come up with the right thing when you knew Carlos better."

Albrecht nodded. "I think I've found the right thing for Carlos. It is – so to speak – a demand that he won't be as **dopey** as I was." He handed him an old single in a faded cover: "Yesterday" by the Beatles. "Whenever you play it, think of the old fool that I am, okay?"

"What do you mean? **It's all double Dutch to me**," replied Carlos, confused.

"If I hadn't been such a hothead, Susanne wouldn't –" Embarrassed, he turned to her and said quietly, "Take care, you two! All the best!"

The guard had to tell us three times to get in. We waved for all we were worth and then, as the train gathered speed, I let the yellow card flutter out of the window at the very last moment.

"End of the adventure on Sylt?" asked Carlos.

"Yes! And the start of new …"

"… adventures together."

---

starfish – Seestern; to be dopey – bekloppt sein; It's all double Dutch to me. – Ich verstehe nur Bahnhof.

Ebenfalls auf Englisch bei Thienemann erschienen:

Sabine Both: *Move to Cloud Nine; Love in my Luggage*
Brinx/Kömmerling: *A Paul to Kiss*
Christamaria Fiedler: *Spaghetti Crime; Risotto Crime*
Sissi Flegel: *Forbidden to Love*
Bianka Minte-König: *Mobile Phone Love; Schoolyard Flirt & Catwalk Dreams*
Hortense Ullrich: *Never Kiss a Witch; Love is Blonde*
Zimmermann & Zimmermann: *Maths, Stress and a Lovesick Heart; School, Trouble & True Love*
Summer, Sun & Holiday Love

Sissi Flegel freut sich über Leserpost: sissi.flegel@gmx.de
Sissi Flegel ist eine Autorin der AVA international GmbH Autoren- und Verlagsagentur, Herrsching (www.ava-international.de).

Flegel, Sissi:
Cool Kisses on the Beach
Aus dem Deutschen von Helena Ragg-Kirkby
ISBN 13: 978 3 522 17934 8

Reihengestaltung: Birgit Schössow
Einbandillustration: Birgit Schössow
Innentypografie: Marlis Killermann
Schrift: Stone serif
Satz: KCS GmbH, Buchholz/Hamburg
Reproduktion: Medienfabrik, Möglingen
Druck und Bindung: Friedrich Pustet, Regensburg

5 4 3 2 1* 07 08 09 10

www.thienemann.de
www.frechemaedchen.de
www.sissi-flegel.de